CLASSIC BUFFALO

A Heritage of Distinguished Architecture

"There is more good architecture in Buffalo – major buildings at the top of their stylistic form – than anyone seems ready to recognize or acknowledge. Architecture is a city's most important and most vulnerable art, and this, tragically, is little understood."

– Ada Louise Huxtable (*New York Times*)

CLASSIC BUFFALO

A Heritage of Distinguished Architecture

Photography by
ANDY OLENICK

Text by
RICHARD O. REISEM

Introduction: Albert L. Michaels
Design: Frank Petronio
Publisher: Joseph F. Bieron
Administration: Janet Leone
Coordination: Sherri Olenick

CANISIUS COLLEGE PRESS

BUFFALO

Page 6: City Hall (1929-1931), 65 Niagara Square, is one of the finest Art Deco public buildings in America. It stands an impressive 32 stories high and, despite its monumental bulk with 566,313 square feet of space, displays a graceful, towering presence. At any moment, you expect Superman to swoop from this futuristic skyscraper facade. The superior design is the work of New York City architect, John J. Wade, who said that the structure "expresses primarily the masculinity, power, and purposeful energy of an industrial community." At the time these words were uttered just before the 1929 stock market crash, Buffalo was a top industrial giant. This remarkable building of gray granite, limestone, and warm sandstone is further adorned with glazed ceramic tiles that add brilliant color to the drum of the tower's glass dome.

Page 4: The elaborate decoration on the building celebrates Buffalo's position when it was called the Queen City of the Lakes. In the carved frieze above the eight huge columns of the main entrance, there are 21 figures tracing Buffalo's preeminence in areas such as transportation, lake shipping, steel, petrochemicals, electricity production, architecture, education, and quality of life for its citizens.

Pages 2-3: The Common Council chamber on the 13th floor of Buffalo City Hall is illuminated by an enormous semi-circular sunburst skylight.

Classic Buffalo

Dedicated to Peter and Elizabeth Tower
whose enthusiasm and generosity
made this book possible.

First published in the United States of America in 1999
by Canisius College Press, Buffalo, NY 14208-1098

Library of Congress Catalog Card Number: 99-074516

ISBN: 0-9671480-0-6

Printed in the U.S.A.
by Canfield & Tack Inc.
Rochester, NY 14608-2802

Contents

Introduction — page 13

Downtown — page 22

Guaranty Building: Louis Sullivan's Masterpiece — page 22

Esenwein and Johnson: An Ideal Partnership — page 38

Delaware Avenue — page 48

The Classic Architecture of Stanford White — page 60

West Side — page 84

H. H. Richardson's Psychiatric Center — page 114

East Side — page 138

E. B. Green, Buffalo's Prolific Architect — page 138

North Buffalo — page 144

Claude Bragdon: Unsung Talent Behind the NYS Pavilion — page 144

The Man Who Brought Frank Lloyd Wright to Buffalo — page 153

South Buffalo — page 162

Joseph Dart's Grain Elevator — page 162

Index — page 172

Bibliography — page 174

Acknowledgments — page 175

Introduction

Buffalo is one of America's most interesting and attractive cities. It has produced two U.S. presidents, numerous stars of the sports and entertainment worlds, and has given birth to a number of important American industries. Today it stands out for the Albright-Knox and Burchfield-Penney art galleries, a world-class hospital system, a major state university and numerous fine small colleges, two major-league sports teams, some of the country's finest restaurants, a diverse and hard-working population, and importantly, as this book demonstrates, marvelous architecture. Buffalo has an abundant water supply, while much of the nation's sunbelt faces serious shortages. And although its economy is currently undergoing serious structural changes, the city has been through difficult times before and Buffalonians are confident in their city's future.

New York Times columnist R.W. Apple described Buffalo as "a dowager in decline who still has good bones to remind people of her more prosperous and glamorous days." This book stands, in a sense, as a tribute to these not so ancient "bones" and their survival. Buffalo's history and architecture are logically intertwined. For without the amazing growth of this small village into a major industrial and commercial center, these buildings would never have been designed and built. Industry and commerce alone provided the funds to hire talent such as Louis Sullivan, H.H. Richardson, Stanford White, and Frank Lloyd Wright to come to Buffalo and create these works that give our city an aesthetic distinction.

It all began in 1825 with the opening of the Erie Canal. The canal created a fast water route from Buffalo to New York City and the Atlantic. It now could take advantage of its location on the eastern shore of Lake Erie and at the mouth of the Niagara River. The city became the logical gateway to America's frontier. It was the start of an incredibly rich commercial and manufacturing economy based on the transport and processing of raw materials. The canal made Buffalo a natural low-cost transfer point for raw materials being developed throughout the Great Lakes region and the rapidly growing Midwest.

In 1832, the state legislature approved Buffalo's newly written charter, and this burgeoning community became a city. A cholera epidemic that year and the bankruptcy in 1837 of its leading entrepreneur, Benjamin Rathbun, did nothing to retard Buffalo's growth.

At first, grain dominated the economy, as shipments began flowing to and from the city. In 1835, Buffalo processed 112,000 bushels of grain. By 1841, the total rose to two million. This process was accelerated by Buffalo inventor, Joseph Dart, who developed the nation's first steam-powered grain elevator. The grain trade led to related manufacturing, and Buffalo became one of the world's leading flour-milling centers as well as the principal transshipment hub.

Commerce created abundant capital which led to further growth; the population increased; churches were built, and crude frame dwellings were replaced by more substantial houses. Grain elevators lined the Buffalo River outlet. The first local entrepreneurs created an economy consisting of shipbuilding, brewing, clothes, leather, furniture, and saddlery. Small foundries began to produce screws, nails, stoves, and boiler engines.

On July 9, 1850, Millard Fillmore, a former Buffalo mayor, became president of the United States. Immigrants, many of them German, began to flood into the boomtown. The population reached 42,261 (from 2,412 in 1825), and the soaring economy expanded into new products.

Iron ore, discovered along the western shores of Lake Superior in 1840, further diversified Buffalo's growing economic base. Iron ore combined with the availability of bituminous coal from western Pennsylvania allowed the manufacture of shovels, hoes, bells, locks, farm machinery, etc.

In 1857, a national depression only briefly slowed Buffalo's momentum. The city, blessed with a growing labor force, national transportation network, local capital, and a rapidly expanding railroad system continued to develop further sources of wealth. The population reached 81,129 in 1860. The same year brought Buffalo's first streetcars. Wealth grew and the banking system developed to channel local capital into new industries. The newly rich entrepreneurs worked vigorously to improve the city's aesthetic environment. Forest Lawn Cemetery (1849), the Historical Society (1862), and Grosvenor

Grain elevator on the Buffalo River front.

Buffalo Lighthouse (1833-1836). Sailors dubbed it "Chinaman's Light, because the top looks like a Chinese hat.

Library (1870) all represent the desire of Buffalo's leading citizens to create a culture appropriate to the city's new economic prominence. Most important, the city government enacted legislation to establish an ambitious new park system. This legislation set the stage for luring to Buffalo a remarkably talented nationally known landscape architect.

Frederick Law Olmsted had designed New York's impressive Central Park. He was in and out of Buffalo between 1870 and 1898, thoroughly redesigning the urban landscape. His local parkway system beautified the city and still today sets the tone for much of its physical appearance.

Among Olmsted's innovations was the use of parkways to connect Buffalo's original radial streets to North Buffalo. His major contribution, however, was Delaware Park. It was Olmsted's attempt to give Buffalonians a pastoral refuge from the city's growing congestion and noise, as well as relief from the general stress of urban living. In 1876, the park was completed. Olmsted also laid out the grounds for a new city and county building (now called Old County Hall). He returned in 1887 to design an ambitious South Buffalo park system. This plan proved too expensive, and he modified it into the 155-acre South Park and the 76-acre Cazenovia Park. The last of Olmsted's five parks in the Buffalo area, the 22-acre Riverside Park, was completed at the end of the century. Olmsted believed that Buffalo had become one of America's best planned urban areas. He proudly exhibited his Buffalo designs at the Philadelphia Centennial and 1878 Paris exhibitions.

Buffalo's location led logically to its becoming a major railroad hub. In 1852, five small local lines were merged into the New York Central system. After 1865, the demands of the lumber industry and the iron ore flowing from Minnesota promoted further rapid railroad growth.

The Interstate Commerce Act of 1887 eliminated rate discrimination and gave further impetus to Buffalo's growing railroad importance. The city became a major center for shipping and processing grain, iron, coal, and cattle products, such as meat and leather goods. The growth of rail lines led to the manufacture of intimately linked products. After 1850, Buffalo produced locomotives, marine engines, rail cars and coaches, wheels for rolling stock, and even railroad bridge-building equipment. The only downside was that the growing importance of railroads began to undermine the significance of the Erie Canal, and shipping tonnage along the canal diminished.

In 1880, Buffalo was both a railroad hub and a major port. The population grew to 155,134. The port of Buffalo's gross tonnage reached 5,935,746. Processing of agricultural products was now central to the region's economic growth. Buffalo mills were producing record amounts of flour. Cicero Hamlin's American Glucose Company listed vast amounts of corn being shipped in from the Midwest. Buffalo breweries also expanded utilizing vast amounts of barley stored in the city's huge elevators. In 1888, nineteen independent breweries operated here.

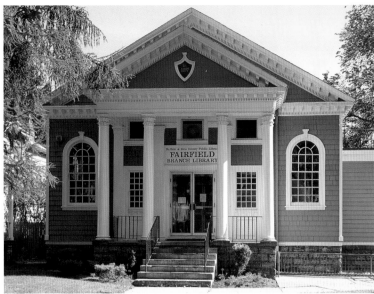

Fairfield Branch Library (1897), 1659 Amherst Street, by William Sydney Wicks.

John D. Larkin opened his manufacturing company in 1875. Fifty years later the Larkin Company became the country's largest mailorder house. Its volume surpassed such retailing giants as Sears Roebuck and Montgomery Ward.

Grover Cleveland, another former mayor, was elected president in 1884.

Progress accelerated throughout the 1890s and Buffalo's future appeared secure. At the turn of the century, Buffalo possessed the two critical factors necessary to add heavy industry to its still expanding base of small manufacturing and commerce: cheap unskilled labor and inexpensive electric power. Niagara Falls hydroelectric power came into use in 1896. By 1898, it had begun to flow to western New York. Everything was in place for an industrial takeoff. The Schoellkopf family played a major role in the development of Niagara Falls power. The family's founder, Jacob F. Schoellkopf, who was in the tanning business, purchased the hydraulic canal in Niagara Falls in 1877 and developed electric power generation. His son, Jacob F. Schoellkopf II, developed a dyestuffs plant in 1880, the first of its kind in America, which evolved into the giant National Aniline and Chemical Company. He continued the family's position as one of the principal owners of regional hydroelectric power and was a major player in Buffalo financial circles. In 1918, Schoellkopf II carried out mergers of small power companies that led to the creation of the Niagara Hudson Power Company which monopolized the electric power utilities along the Niagara River. Schoellkopf, John J. Albright, John Milburn, William Hoyt, and other leading citizens used the advantages of Buffalo's new power sources to persuade Lackawanna Steel Company to relocate to western New York from Scranton, Pennsylvania.

In the 19th century, steel was largely produced in small mills located throughout Pennsylvania. The industry's owners realized that operations and profits would be enhanced if they could integrate their plants to combine ironmaking, steel production, coke ovens, and rolling mills in one location. The lake region around Buffalo was perfect for this kind of operation. Lackawanna Steel opened its large Buffalo plant in 1905. The plant immediately created 6,000 new jobs. Soon after, Cleveland-based Republic Steel came to the region. These two plants and other smaller companies made Buffalo a potential rival to Pittsburgh as the steelmaking capital of the United States.

In 1900, Buffalo's population reached 352,387. Major building construction now began to transform the urban landscape into today's classic Buffalo. The Dun Building went up in 1894. In the following year, Stanford White came to Buffalo to design the Williams-Butler mansion on Delaware Avenue. The Guaranty and Ellicott Square buildings followed in 1895 and 1896. The former, designed by Louis Sullivan, has been called America's "first skyscraper masterpiece." The Ellicott Square Building was, at the turn of the century, the world's largest office building. It held 600 separate offices. Darwin D. Martin, an executive at the Larkin Soap Company, brought architect Frank Lloyd Wright to Buffalo and persuaded John D. Larkin, the company's president, to commission Wright to design a new administration building. Completed in 1904, it was

Forest Lawn Cemetery mausoleums.

probably the world's most innovative office design. Wright subsequently returned to design six houses in the area including the internationally acclaimed Darwin D. Martin House. The Albright Gallery, in contrast to Wright's futuristic designs, harkened back to ancient Greece for its style inspiration and opened in 1905.

In 1900, Buffalo surpassed Chicago as the greatest city on the Great Lakes. Buffalo was the nation's largest inland port; only six international ports exceeded its trade volume, and Buffalo was still growing. Buffalo was second to Chicago nationally as a rail and livestock-processing center, but Buffalo had a more diversified and innovative economic base. A New York Times journalist wrote in 1879 that if Buffalo secured its trade from the canal and kept growing, "then Buffalo and not Chicago would be the second American city." Within a quarter of a century, Buffalo also rivaled Detroit for automotive manufacturing, Pittsburgh for steelmaking, and equaled Minneapolis as a milling center. In these same years, the city became a national base for the fledgling aircraft and chemical industries.

The Pan-American Exposition opened in Buffalo on May 1, 1901. Its local backers hoped to make money. They also saw the world's fair as an opportunity to enhance the international reputation of Buffalo's growing prosperity. Visitors could view many marvels including a 400-foot-high electric tower lighted by 11,000 colored lights which bystanders compared to diamonds, sapphires, and rubies. Tourists could also visit an Indian village, watch bullfights, and listen to concerts by the Mexican Royal Artillery Band. But the exposition was not a success. Marred by poor weather from May through July, labor disputes, the assassination of President William McKinley, and cost overruns, it lost its backers some $6 million. The only structure to survive on its original site was the handsome, but traditionally neoclassical New York State pavilion, which became the Buffalo and Erie County Historical Society.

Although the exposition proved to be a disappointment, Buffalo's morale remained boosterish. The port thrived; the railroad industry was still growing, and the city remained a center for the storage and processing of midwestern wheat, corn, and other grains. Buffalo's businessmen kept opening new plants which took advantage of cheap power, a central location, and a steadily growing immigrant labor force.

In 1914, the construction of the Concrete Central elevator gave Buffalo the world's largest grain elevator at the time. Meanwhile, the fledgling industries of aviation, automobiles, and chemicals all expanded in the area. Buffalo's banks were consolidating and growing, creating even higher salaries for bankers and providing a potential source of capital for more economic diversification.

Immigrant communities contained charming cottages.

Buffalo's diverse and talented population also promoted economic growth. Its elite, still mainly white Anglo-Saxon Protestant with a mixture of Germans and western European Jews, generously contributed to the city's growing cultural infrastructure. The Albright Art Gallery, as well as the city's historical society, philharmonic orchestra, and science museum all stood as side effects of the region's economic growth. Buffalo's newly rich hired nationally famous architects to build both residentially and commercially. The Buffalo Society of Artists and the Albright Art School contributed to a thriving artistic community, and by the 1920s the city could boast of many lavish movie theaters. Shea's Buffalo Theatre opened in 1926. The immigrant communities – German, Irish, Italian, Polish, and eastern European Jewish – found jobs and opportunities for their children. A large number of African-Americans moved to the city in the 1940s and obtained work in war industries, but they suffered more than any other group from Buffalo's subsequent decline.

The steel industry, located in nearby Lackawanna, became critical to the health of the region's economy. Bethlehem Steel purchased Lackawanna Steel in 1922 and expanded its facilities. Republic Steel enlarged its operations, and several medium-sized companies also settled in western New York. The Depression reduced profits and employment, but then World War II reversed the decline. During the war, Bethlehem-Lackawanna became the world's largest steelmaking operation. It employed 20,000 workers on a 1,300-acre site. Changing technologies, rising labor costs, competition, and geographical shifts in transportation and industrial patterns eventually terminated Lackawanna's steel production in 1982. Its closing was a devastating blow to the local economy.

Thirty independent automobile companies operated in Buffalo during the first quarter of the 20th century, among them the Kensington, the Babcock Electric, and the Pierce. The two most famous were Thomas Flyer and Pierce-Arrow. In 1908, the Flyer took first place in a 16,000-mile race from New York to Paris. During this 16-month trip, the cars traveled the primitive roads of western U.S., Siberia, and eastern Europe. The Pierce-Arrow was the best constructed, fastest, most luxurious and expensive automobile in the early days of the industry. When other cars did well to go 15 mph, the Pierce-Arrow could do 60. The E.R. Thomas Motor Company closed because of inefficient marketing and a basically uncompetitive style. The Pierce-Arrow was too expensive to produce.

Pioneer aircraft companies also located in western New York. Curtiss-Wright operated the world's largest aircraft plant in Buffalo during World War I. At that time it employed 3,000 workers who produced 150 planes a year. Later, Bell Aircraft opened in the nearby town of Wheatfield. Before moving to Texas in the 1960s, Bell built one of the first American jets and the first aircraft to break the sound barrier. It also pioneered in the development of the helicopter. Again, technological changes in the industry, management turnovers, and the high cost of manufacturing in New York State caused this industry either to close or depart from the region.

Edward Duerr House (1927), 181 Depew Avenue, was designed by Eli Goldstein in Churrigueresque Baroque style, inspired by architecture at the 1901 Pan-American Exposition.

In 1929, the city's two most luxurious apartment complexes, the Campanile and 800 West Ferry, opened their doors. The Buffalo Museum of Science, the Vars Building, and City Hall were all in the process of construction. A municipal airport began operating in 1927. The city, then still the center of the airplane industry, had an airport long before most other American cities.

The Depression hit Buffalo hard. But even earlier, the Buffalo economy began to exhibit serious flaws. In the 1920s, outside companies began to control most of Buffalo's newer and more dynamic enterprises. The owners of industries – such as steel, aircraft, autos, and oil refining – were not generally from Buffalo. They rarely visited the city. Understandably, their interest was chiefly in profits and not the aesthetic environment. So later, it was easy for them to divest or close down branches in a community to which they felt little loyalty. The nineteen breweries were largely locally owned, but they were undermined by Prohibition. Several of the large chemical companies located in Niagara Falls had only minimal impact on the city of Buffalo. The railroads had been eroded by the automobile and also by federal rate changes making it more expensive to move goods in and out of Buffalo. Many in the Buffalo elite had invested their capital in railroad bonds whose value declined throughout the 1920s. This in turn reduced the amount of capital available to the region. Some statistics were worrying. Population growth began to slow. Between 1910 and 1920, the population rose 19 percent, while over the next ten years it slowed to 13 percent. Auto firms closed. Pierce-Arrow, the pride of the community, was purchased by Studebaker. By 1930, the city's chief rivals, Detroit and Cleveland, surpassed Buffalo in population and economic output.

Then the Depression delivered a devastating blow. In 1930, unemployment reached 20 percent. By 1936, 25 percent of the community's families lived on federal relief. In 1937, western New York steel plants were operating at 18 percent of capacity. Pierce-Arrow closed in 1937 leaving 1,000 workers unemployed. One of the few bright spots was the opening in 1940 of Kleinhans Music Hall, one of the acoustically finest such auditoriums in the world.

Historian Mark Goldman described World War II as the "best thing that happened to Buffalo" at this critical time. Congress repealed the Arms Embargo Act in 1934, and the effect on Buffalo's heavy industry was almost immediate. Steel, aircraft, and their allied products took on new workers and increased production. Once again, the future looked promising.

Goldman also pointed out that the Depression and the World War II economic recovery forever changed the dynamics of Buffalo's economy. Prior to 1930, economic growth had been largely autonomous. It depended on location, electric power, an entrepreneurial spirit, and the skills and willingness to work of Buffalo's labor force. After 1930, Buffalo became increasingly tied to Washington. Depression relief funds and, later, wartime orders literally saved Buffalo. Added to this was the fact that its major industrial base was increasingly controlled by outside interests. The old families – the Goodyears, Jewetts, Knoxes, Rands, Rumseys, and Schoellkopfs – still existed but their influence on Buffalo's economy was greatly reduced. Buffalo no longer controlled its own destiny.

Kleinhans Music Hall by Eliel and Eero Saarinen opened in 1940.

Buffalo slumped again after the war's end, but then appeared to recover. In 1951, the popular Saturday Evening Post called Buffalo, "a city with futures unlimited." The article advised "any man who can build a better mousetrap might be smart to spurn Emerson's stay-home advice and instead shuffle off to Buffalo." Buffalo was still the fifteenth biggest city in the U.S. Its banking industry had grown. Steel and auto parts manufacturing flourished in Lackawanna. Buffalo mills performed 77 percent of the nation's grain milling. In 1954, Buffalo was still the country's largest inland port and the twelfth largest port overall. It was still the second largest rail hub in the U.S., however, railroad business had declined. And it was the country's sixth largest steel producer, the eighth largest manufacturing center, and one of the world's greatest flour and animal-feed milling centers.

But a decade later, the picture had deteriorated. The city's population had declined. Buffalo was America's 29th largest city in 1970 and 36th in 1980. The port was underutilized, in fact, almost dormant. Republic and Bethlehem had virtually closed their steelmaking facilities. Local manufacturing and downtown retailing were barely visible. Railroads were of little importance. The automotive parts sector was still thriving in Lackawanna but dependent on outside ownership. The education system needed attention. Unable to find jobs, educated youth began to leave. There seemed to be few lights at the end of Buffalo's long tunnel. There were still, however, the buildings of classic Buffalo to remind residents of better days and provide inspiration for their return.

Buffalo's decline has been severe, but it is not terminal. It remains to review some of the factors that explain Buffalo's descent from an industrial giant to a depressed city. Many other older cities in northeast and upper midwest U.S. suffered the current urban crisis; they simply were not equipped to cope with the unknown and unknowable economic problems that lay ahead after World War II. Some, like Cleveland and Pittsburgh, recovered. Buffalo has not – yet. One factor was the lack of a U.S. Senator from western New York for the last 53 years. Another was local political leadership.

Just before the Depression, at the height of Buffalo's prosperity and when optimism reigned everywhere, the city began the construction of a new immense city hall. The architect, John J. Wade, said that the building expressed the masculinity, power, and purposeful energy of a highly successful industrial community. It was an impressive 32 stories high and contained an incredible more than half a million square feet of space. The natural inclination was to fill the enormous space with employees, and that was not a problem when the city's tax base was equally enormous and growing.

But when the city declined, the vast bureaucracy did not respond with the vision, imagination, and leadership that was required in such critical times. But not all of Buffalo's decline can be traced to failures of local politicians.

Temple Beth Zion (1966-1967) at 805 Delaware Avenue was designed by Harrison and Abramovitz with a marvelous window by Ben Shahn.

Centerpointe, Essjay Road, Williamsville, was built by Ciminelli Development in 1987-1999.

Since 1900, the city depended on capital-intensive industry and related enterprises: steel, automotive equipment and parts, electrical equipment, chemicals, bulk storage of western grain, milling, industrial machinery, and printing. Local prosperity and employment were dependent on these industries. Rising energy and labor costs, federal regulations, environmental pollution controls, and burdensome taxes combined to make these industries extremely vulnerable to foreign competition. Yet some of these same industries have relocated within the United States and prospered. In 1992, Hooker Chemical chose the state of Mississippi over Niagara Falls as the site of a new chlorine plant. The company explained that its choice was dictated by a combination of costs for land, the labor situation, and the cost of doing business in New York State. Bethlehem Steel's president blamed massive layoffs in 1991 on oppressive taxes, unrealistic environmental control laws, and an uncooperative labor force.

New York State has been another factor in Buffalo's decline. According to a 1998 article in the Buffalo News, the city has the nation's highest tax burden. State and local taxes paid by Buffalo residents are the highest of 100 U.S. metropolitan areas surveyed by the Kiplinger Letter.

The opening of the Saint Lawrence Seaway in 1958 further contributed to Buffalo's situation. Ocean-going vessels carrying products to and from the Midwest now bypassed the city. In the seaway's first year, grain shipments dropped 45 percent below the average of the preceding 25 years. Rapidly, Buffalo's waterfront industries closed, and the local grain-storage operations went into decline. The seaway essentially took away what had been given to Buffalo by the Erie Canal.

Buffalo has continually been depicted in the national media as a chilly, forbidding place, buried for substantial periods under snow. Only the Sunbelt benefits from this unjustified mockery. Buffalo enjoys many advantages over other parts of the U.S. Hurricanes that devastate eastern and southern coastal cities can't possibly reach it. Nor is it a tornado alley like so much of the midwest. Earthquakes here are very rare and if at all, extremely minor tremors. And smog? Inconceivable in this clean city with gentle breezes. The city has more sunny days than Seattle; winter temperatures are milder than midwest cities; summers are superior to any place in the Sunbelt, and Buffalo's snowfall is either matched or exceeded in locations across half of the U.S.

There are other factors that affect Buffalo's recent condition. Unions have driven up labor costs. Suburbs have drained the city of economic activity. A major-league football stadium and the State University of New York were both recently located outside the city limits, further depriving it of economic vitality.

Architect Frederic K. Houston designed his own family residence at 1000 Willardshire Road, East Aurora, in 1970-1989.

HSBC Center adds contemporary style to downtown Buffalo.

Most of the architecture celebrated in this book went up before World War II during Buffalo's period of incredible prosperity. Yet despite Buffalo's decline, exciting new well designed structures are being erected that improve the landscape, create a more desirable environment, and give evidence that Buffalo still has a future. Buffalo's rich may no longer be bringing in the likes of H. H. Richardson, Stanford White, and Frank Lloyd Wright to build their personal residences, but banks, corporations, and the government have all recently imported nationally known architects to build commercial office buildings, educational institutions, and government buildings.

Many new buildings are controversial because some Buffalonians believe modern styles meld poorly with older structures that for so long have defined Buffalo's skyline. Every age seems to share such feelings when new styles make an appearance. Erie County Savings Bank, HSBC Bank, and Manufacturers and Traders Trust Company all constructed major headquarters buildings in contemporary styles. The most notable and least controversial is One M&T Plaza designed by Minoru Yamasaki. The Buffalo News engaged Edward Durrell Stone to build its headquarters. Local government has commissioned a number of modernist structures including the Rath Building and the new City Courthouse. The state hired such internationally known architects as Marcel Breuer, Ulrich Franzen, and I. M. Pei to design buildings on the State University of New York's Amherst campus. Results are debatable. The Buffalo Bisons playing field is an excellent example of postmodernism. In this case, Buffalonians are pleased with a stadium that they regard as both functional and attractive. In Amherst, the Ciminelli Company has constructed Centerpointe Development, which adds architectural style to an otherwise undistinguished suburban environment. Residential architecture has also blossomed with innovative development such as River Mist in the city along the Niagara River and with individual private homes in suburbs like East Aurora.

Buffalo is undergoing changes, but it is still a marvelous place in which to live. Donald Clark, president of the National Education Association of New York, pointed out in a 1988 Buffalo News editorial that the city has an excellent reputation for health care, environment, transportation, the arts, and recreation. He wrote, "People who are productively employed in the metro area enjoy a quality of life second to none in the U.S." Buffalo has problems, but its architecture, universities and colleges, museums, restaurants, sports teams, and medical facilities combine to make it a wonderful place to live and bring up children.

It is the architecture of this "wonderful place to live" that is the subject of this handsome book. May it be the inspiration from the past for a bright future.

Albert L. Michaels, Ph.D.
September, 1999

Guaranty Building: Louis Sullivan's Masterpiece

The highest recognition and honor a building can achieve in the United States is the designation, National Historic Landmark. The Guaranty Building, built in 1894-1895, was so designated in 1975. It is nationally regarded as a milestone in modern skyscraper architecture, and Chicago architect Louis Henri Sullivan was its creator. With its refined and elaborately decorated terra-cotta exterior, the building is not only supremely handsome, but its inner structure of steel support with applied exterior curtain walls was a major innovation from wall-supported structures that were the only way to build since before the Greeks. The breakthrough started by architects like Louis Sullivan led to the great American invention, the skyscraper.

Louis Sullivan (1856-1924) studied architecture at Massachusetts Institute of Technology and the Ecole des Beaux Arts in Paris. In 1879, he joined the architecture firm of brilliant Dankmar Adler in Chicago. Sullivan became the leader of the famous Chicago School of architects. He developed an organic theory, which he described in three words, "Form follows function," which may sound obvious today, but was highly original in the latter part of the 19th century.

As American cities and industry grew, so did office buildings, which wanted to be in the thick of things, and that meant an urban setting. Owners of such buildings, therefore, wanted to get the most out of crowded, valuable downtown sites. This, in turn, created a demand for taller buildings. Historically, there were two limitations that restricted the height of buildings. One involved vertical transportation, which was solved in the 1860s by the invention of the modern elevator. The second concerned the structural system, which limited building heights by the number of stones or bricks that could be stacked on top of one another without having impracticably thick walls. By 1890, steel was being mass produced, and it permitted a strong, slender skeleton that could support itself, the weight of many floors, and a thin, light curtain wall for weatherproofing. The remaining challenge was to make the end result aesthetically pleasing. Louis Sullivan was the first with the best solution. His skyscrapers looked tall, proud, and soaring.

Consider the Guaranty Building, one of the earliest skyscrapers and certainly one of the most handsome. Vertical shafts of piers soar uninterrupted past multiple, uniform office floors to be capped by a row of oculus windows and a mighty cornice. The whole has the elegance of a rectangular fluted column. Then, to give the building its final exuberance, Sullivan sheathed it in lively, reddish-brown terra cotta that is ornamented with elaborate designs.

The Guaranty Building clearly shows Louis Sullivan to be the most competent architect of his period and is a treasured masterpiece on Buffalo's urban landscape.

Fine metalwork on the interior of the Guaranty Building reflects the elaborate designs of the exterior facade. A fire in 1974 severely damaged upper floors, and the building was almost razed. It was superbly restored, fortunately, at a cost of more than $8 million, making the building a jewel in Buffalo's downtown. It is a National Historic Landmark.

Opposite page and above: Guaranty Building (1894-1895), 28 Church Street, is a world-famous masterpiece by Chicago architect Louis Sullivan. Buffalo developer Hascal Taylor wanted the finest office building in the city and commissioned Sullivan to design it. But Taylor died before construction started, so the Guaranty Construction Company, which Taylor had hired to build the new skyscraper, undertook the project themselves and, being the owner, named it the Guaranty Building. Then, two years later, the Prudential Insurance Company assumed the financing of the building and attached its name to it. After Prudential sold the building and restoration occurred, the name reverted to that of the original owner. Narrow piers separating the windows give an upward thrust to this outstanding example of one of America's first sky-scrapers. The piers draw the eye upward to a row of bull's-eye windows and a strong, projecting cornice. Sullivan's consummate skill made a huge 13-story box look graceful and soaring. Red terra cotta tiles cover the facade in a warm, inviting color and are lavishly decorated with intricate geometric shapes.

Following pages: When viewing architecture, it is usually rewarding to look up. This is the sublime illuminated stained-glass ceiling of the Guaranty Building lobby.

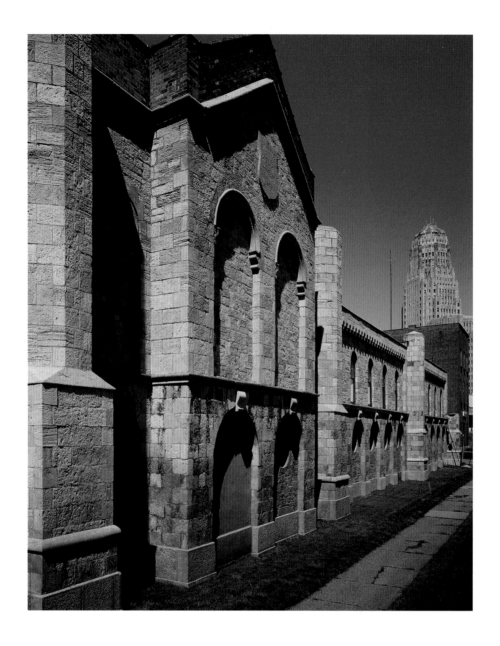

Above: Illuminating Gas Company (1848-1859), 249 West Genesee Street, was started in 1848 on this site near the Erie Basin where it received deliveries of coal for the manufacture of illuminating gas. The 250-foot-long stone facade shown here was built in 1859 from a design by John H. Selkirk (1808-1878), who was both a Buffalo architect and a builder. He designed and erected many houses, churches, and commercial buildings in early Buffalo, including his last work, Asbury United Methodist Church (1876), 80 West Tupper Street. The Illuminating Gas Company's main building, constructed to resemble a fortress but a ruins today, is in the National Register of Historic Places.

Right: Old County Hall (1871-1876), 92 Franklin Street, dominated Buffalo's late 19th-century skyline. It was designed by the prolific Rochester architect, Andrew Jackson Warner, to consolidate the functions of city and county governments at that time. The monumental building was built of granite from Clarke's Island, Maine, and the interior contained offices and courtrooms in handsomely detailed black walnut with floors of fine marble. The building has Gothic-style pointed gables and Romanesque-style rounded arches above the windows; Warner described the style as Norman. The most striking feature of the building is the magnificent 268-foot clock tower. One writer commented, "It is somewhat a fatiguing experience to climb up the narrow staircase, but whoever does so will be well repaid by an examination of the complicated clock mechanism. The dials are in reality nine feet in diameter. Directly above the clock (which has four faces) is a lantern or observatory." Originally, 28 more clocks in the building ran off the master in the tower. Four solid-granite statues, each 16 feet high and weighing 14 tons, decorate the four corners of the tower.

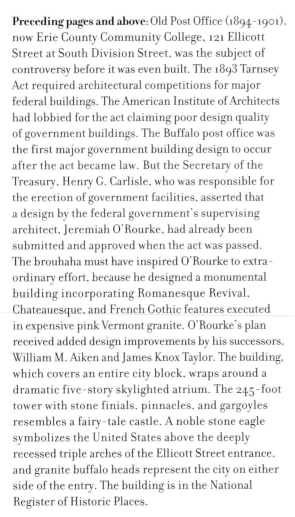

Preceding pages and above: Old Post Office (1894-1901), now Erie County Community College, 121 Ellicott Street at South Division Street, was the subject of controversy before it was even built. The 1893 Tarnsey Act required architectural competitions for major federal buildings. The American Institute of Architects had lobbied for the act claiming poor design quality of government buildings. The Buffalo post office was the first major government building design to occur after the act became law. But the Secretary of the Treasury, Henry G. Carlisle, who was responsible for the erection of government facilities, asserted that a design by the federal government's supervising architect, Jeremiah O'Rourke, had already been submitted and approved when the act was passed. The brouhaha must have inspired O'Rourke to extraordinary effort, because he designed a monumental building incorporating Romanesque Revival, Chateauesque, and French Gothic features executed in expensive pink Vermont granite. O'Rourke's plan received added design improvements by his successors, William M. Aiken and James Knox Taylor. The building, which covers an entire city block, wraps around a dramatic five-story skylighted atrium. The 245-foot tower with stone finials, pinnacles, and gargoyles resembles a fairy-tale castle. A noble stone eagle symbolizes the United States above the deeply recessed triple arches of the Ellicott Street entrance, and granite buffalo heads represent the city on either side of the entry. The building is in the National Register of Historic Places.

Right page: St. Paul's Episcopal Cathedral (1849-1851), Church and Pearl streets, was designed by America's foremost architect of the Gothic Revival style, Richard Upjohn of New York City. It was designated a National Historic Landmark in 1987. Upjohn considered this his most successful design. He had the amazing ability to erect a large Gothic-style cathedral that is asymmetrical in plan and elevation and place it all on a very limited, irregular site, yet making it striking and handsome. It is built of Medina sandstone, a warm reddish stone native to western New York State and quarried at Hulberton in Orleans County. Upjohn came to America from England as a young man, and in designing St. Paul's, he incorporated ideas from 13th-century churches of his youth in rural England. A gas explosion and fire in 1888 gutted the church, and the interior was rebuilt from a revised design by Robert W. Gibson. But the exterior is still all Upjohn. The main steeple is 270 feet high, competing effectively with nearby skyscrapers of more than 20 stories. With its lancet windows, pointed arches, pinnacles, crockets, buttresses, drip moldings, steep gables, and tracery, St. Paul's is much more interesting to look at than many of the skyscrapers.

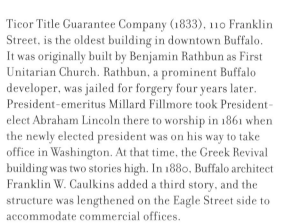

Ticor Title Guarantee Company (1833), 110 Franklin Street, is the oldest building in downtown Buffalo. It was originally built by Benjamin Rathbun as First Unitarian Church. Rathbun, a prominent Buffalo developer, was jailed for forgery four years later. President-emeritus Millard Fillmore took President-elect Abraham Lincoln there to worship in 1861 when the newly elected president was on his way to take office in Washington. At that time, the Greek Revival building was two stories high. In 1880, Buffalo architect Franklin W. Caulkins added a third story, and the structure was lengthened on the Eagle Street side to accommodate commercial offices.

Lafayette Hotel (1901-1904), 391 Washington Street, was designed by Louise Blanchard Bethune (1856-1913), the first professional woman architect in the U.S. and the first woman accepted for membership in the American Institute of Architects. She studied at Cornell University and worked for five years in the architectural firm of Richard A. Waite and F. W. Caulkins before becoming a partner with her architect husband, Robert Bethune. In its heyday, the Lafayette Hotel was considered one of the 15 finest hotels in the country. Built in French Baroque style, it boasted crystal ballrooms, leaded-glass skylights, marble columns, and mahogany coatrooms.

Right: Liberty Building (1925), 424 Main Street, was designed by the New York skyscraper architect Alfred Bossom (1881-1965). He liked to decorate the tops of his tall buildings with romantic symbols. For this 23-story structure, originally the Liberty Bank Building, he selected twin, 30-foot bronze replicas of the Statue of Liberty. One faces east, the other, west. To Bossom, they were symbols of Buffalo's strategic position in the country, being the western outpost of the East and the East's gateway to the West.

Above: Dennis (now, Stanton) Building (circa 1873), 251-257 Main Street, is the only surviving structure in Buffalo to have the entire five-story facade made of cast iron. The idea was to mold all of the decorative elements – columns, pilasters, capitals, arched window lintels, dentil moldings, and cornices – out of iron and then paint the iron to resemble stone. As quality stone became more expensive, cast iron was an economical alternative that produced a similar effect. In the latter half of the 19th and first half of the 20th centuries, Buffalo was a major producer of iron and steel, and several large architectural ironwork firms existed here after 1850. Iron ore came from the upper Great Lakes, and coal to fire the blast furnaces came from Pennsylvania. They met in Buffalo to make iron and steel.

Right: Dun Building (1894-1895), 110 Pearl Street, was designed by E. B. Green and William S. Wicks, who applied the Neoclassical style of horizontal buildings to a vertical tower, so the facade is divided into a series of multiple-story bands stacked one on top of the other. The central band shown here features giant four-story window arches, decoratively framed oval windows on the seventh floor, and other architectural details that are more interesting than those on the bands below and above it. Although the building has a supporting steel skeleton, the walls also had to be made load-bearing to give the very narrow structure more bracing against the strong winds off Lake Erie. The building was named for the R. G. Dun Company, which later became Dun and Bradstreet. At 10 stories, it was the first Buffalo highrise.

Esenwein and Johnson: An Ideal Partnership

August Carl Esenwein (1856-1926) and James Addison Johnson (1865-1939) made an ideal architectural team. Esenwein was solidly trained in Europe and besides being a highly competent architect, he was an excellent salesman for his design ideas. When General Electric wanted a four- or five-story modest office building, Esenwein sold them a dramatic 20-story gleaming white skyscraper. Johnson, trained at McKim, Mead & White in New York City, followed in the footsteps of Stanford White in his devotion to outstanding ornament. It was James Johnson who designed the spectacular marble mosaic floor of the Ellicott Square Building.

Esenwein was born in Germany in 1856, and, before coming to Buffalo in 1880, studied architecture in Paris, the world center for architectural theory and education at that time. He was a prime mover of the 1901 Pan-American Exposition and served on its board of eight architects. Esenwein and Johnson designed the Temple of Music where President William McKinley was assassinated.

Johnson was an American, born in Brewerton, New York in 1865 and educated in the U.S. His first architectural practice was as an assistant at the New York firm of McKim, Mead & White. He was 32 years old when he formed a partnership with Esenwein in 1897, a relationship that continued for 29 years until Esenwein died in 1926. Their offices were in the Ellicott Square Building.

Together, Esenwein and Johnson designed, among many others, the highly ornamented Calumet Building at 46-58 West Chippewa Street, the Niagara Mohawk Building (originally General Electric Tower), 535 Washington Street, with Johnson's unusual decorative motifs featuring electric motors and generators (precursors of Art Deco), the small but refined neoclassical building at 620 Main Street, the Ansonia Building in Art Nouveau style at 712-726 Main Street, the elaborate Thomas J. McKinney House at 35 Lincoln Parkway, the Col. Francis G. Ward Pumping Station (largest in the world in its day) at the end of Porter Avenue, the refined Alexander Main Curtiss House at 780 West Ferry Avenue, the landmark Lafayette High School at 370 Lafayette Avenue, the elaborately decorated Jewett House at 313 Summer Street, and the elegant Buffalo Museum of Science at 1020 Humboldt Parkway.

Left: Ansonia Building (1921), 712-726 Main Street, was designed by Esenwein and Johnson for commercial use. The facade in Art Nouveau style is covered in glazed cream-and-green terra cotta. The deep cavetto cornice is decorated with an unusual tree motif on the tiles, which is the work of architect partner and master ornamentalist, James Addison Johnson.

Right: Niagara Mohawk Building (1912), 535 Washington Street, was originally called General Electric Tower. The prominent Buffalo architectural firm of August Carl Esenwein and James Addison Johnson, inspired by the Electric Tower at the Pan-American Exposition in 1901, created a slender octagonal 294-foot-high skyscraper sheathed in white-glazed terra cotta that makes it gleam after every rainfall. On top of the 14-story office building there is a three-tiered tower, looking very much like a white-frosted wedding cake in both daylight and floodlight.

Ellicott Square Building (1895-1896), 295 Main Street, occupies an entire large city block. When built, it was the largest office building in the world. Joseph Ellicott, founder of Buffalo (although as agent for the Holland Land Company, he worked hard to have it called New Amsterdam), had reserved this site for his private estate, but he resigned from the Holland Land Company in 1821 and later moved to New York City where he committed suicide in 1826. When an office building was planned for the site, the owners hired Chicago architect Daniel Burnham to design it. "Make no little plans," Burnham told the owners, "they have no magic to stir men's blood." Blood continues to be stirred daily in those who enter this remarkable building. From both Main and Washington streets, people pass through identical entrances formed by triumphal Roman arches flanked by heavily grooved and banded columns.

Right: Once inside the Ellicott Square Building, people face a giant atrium covered by an immense, elaborately structured skylight. The inlaid marble floor, installed in 1929 from a design by James Addison Johnson of Esenwein and Johnson (who had their offices in the building), depicts sun symbols from civilizations around the world, and a sweeping wrought-iron stairway leads to a second-floor balcony with a highly decorative iron balustrade. Although Burnham was the supervising architect, it was Charles B. Atwood, chief designer of the Chicago Columbian Exposition and master of artistic matters at D. H. Burnham & Company, who conceived the elaborate exterior and interior decoration of this 10-story Italian Renaissance building.

Above and left: Market Arcade (1892), 617 Main Street, is the Buffalo version of the Burlington Arcade on Piccadilly in London. G. B. Marshall commissioned E. B. Green to design the building and suggested that Green study the Burlington Arcade for inspiration. The arcade of interior shops along a common hallway is two stories high and extends between Main and Washington streets. A third floor provides office space. The two street facades are clad in yellow Roman brick with complex terra cotta decoration. Double columns on either side of the entrance support a huge Roman arch with six bands of intricately carved classical moldings, each distinctly different from the others. The keystone of the arch is an elaborate design incorporating the carved head of a buffalo.

Right: Buffalo Savings Bank (1900-1901), 545 Main Street, which originally had a copper roof, now possesses a brilliantly gilded ceramic-tile dome. Even the 15-foot-high finial has a coating of gold leaf. E. B. Green and William S. Wicks won the competition to design the building, and inspired by the 1893 World's Columbian Exposition in Chicago, they created a neo-classical bank of regal stature.

Above: Shea's Center for the Performing Arts (1926), 646 Main Street, was originally a movie palace, one of the finest in the country. It takes its name from Michael Shea, the most significant theater operator in the history of Buffalo. His company operated a chain of theaters throughout the metropolitan area, but this was his flagship. The architects were Cornelius W. and George W. Rapp of Chicago. They were Paramount's house architects and among the most distinguished theater designers of their time. To the left is Theatre Place (1896), 636-644 Main Street, which was originally designed for Delia L. Root to house retail stores. The Beaux Arts style building was designed by Buffalo architect, Edward A. Kent.

Left: The 3,183-seat Shea's theater has an opulent, French Baroque interior, a grand lobby lined with marble and mirrors. The ornate chandeliers are of Czech glass.

Following pages: In 1925, Louis Comfort Tiffany, 78 years old at the time, submitted to the Rapps an interior design for Shea's Buffalo. The architects used a portion of the design but preferred their own ideas for much of the lavish interior. The excitement was not only in the architecture, because it was here where the great films of Hollywood's golden age were shown. Between the multiple daily film showings, there was a stage show with a full orchestra and performances on the monumental Wurlitzer pipe organ made in nearby North Tonawanda. Shea's is in the National Register of Historic Places.

Above and right: Trinity Episcopal Church (1884-1886), 371 Delaware Avenue, was originally designed by Arthur Gilman of Boston, but only Christ Chapel and the foundation for the rest of the church were built in 1869. Several years later, Buffalo architect Cyrus K. Porter prepared a revised design, which was constructed between 1884 and 1886. The spire, however, was never built. The truly outstanding features of Trinity Church are its stained-glass windows designed by John LaFarge, who developed a whole new industry of glassmaking in America based on creating a spectacular array of effects with glass alone, without using paint. He developed a new method of manufacturing semi-translucent glass that simulated painted effects. His windows for Trinity Church are among the best LaFarge ever created and are recognized as some of the finest stained glass in America. The Watson window over the altar in the north transept is called *The Sealing of the Twelve Tribes* described in Revelation, Chapter 7. The window won the highest honor at the 1889 Exposition Universale in Paris, where it was shown before being installed in Trinity Church. Five windows in the apse and the magnificent rose window in the sanctuary are also by LaFarge. Other windows, equally superb, were designed by Louis Comfort Tiffany.

Following pages: Stephen Van Rensselaer Watson House (now, Buffalo Club) (1870), 388 Delaware Avenue, was designed in Second Empire style for the founder of the Erie County Savings Bank. It was Watson's wife who commissioned John LaFarge to create *The Sealing of the Twelve Tribes* stained-glass window in Trinity Episcopal Church across the street. The Buffalo Club moved here in 1887. It had been founded 20 years earlier on January 2, 1867 with Millard Fillmore as the club's first president. When President William McKinley was assassinated at the Pan-American Exposition in 1901, the Buffalo Club invited McKinley's White House administration to make the club's commodious facilities its temporary headquarters during the president's terminal illness. The lobby of the Buffalo Club was originally the reception hall of the Stephen Van Rensselaer Watson House. Rexford Tugwell, one of President Franklin Roosevelt's aides, described the Buffalo Club as "the resort of the wealthy, powerful, uncontaminated conservatives of the business community – a regional center of capitalism at its time of most unlimited power." It is the only club of its kind to have had two U.S. presidents as members, Millard Fillmore and Grover Cleveland.

Above: William E. Dorsheimer House (1868-1871), 434-438 Delaware Avenue, was designed by Henry Hobson Richardson when he was a young, 30-year-old architect with only three years of architectural practice. He adapted a French style that he had studied in Paris. It involved placing horizontal bands of gray sandstone across the ochre brick facade and vertical stone courses at the building corners. Windows on the three-story structure are also framed by vertical bands of sandstone and are stacked in orderly perpendicular rows. The slate mansard roof has large dormers lending a picturesque quality to an otherwise relatively plain house. When the building was converted to offices in the 1950s, it was defaced in a number of ways including the removal of ornate iron cresting above bay window and porch areas. It was in this house that Dorsheimer, Pascal Pratt, and other Buffalo parks commissioners first met with the great American landscape architect, Frederick Law Olmsted, to plan a park system for the city. The house is included in the National Register of Historic Places.

Right: Statler Towers (1921-1923), 107 Delaware Avenue, is comprised of three 19-story brick-and-stone towers joined at the bottom by a red brick and gray stone base. Previously on the site was U.S. President Millard Fillmore's mansion, which was demolished to make way for Ellsworth Statler's grandest hotel in the U.S. It has been converted to offices today. The building was designed by New York architects, George B. Post & Sons, in English Renaissance Revival style.

Preceding pages and at right: The Midway (1889-1895), 471-499 Delaware Avenue, is comprised of neoclassical row houses that extend for one long city block. Row houses, while quite common in east coast cities, were rare in the wide open spaces of the western New York State city of Buffalo. With ample land available inexpensively, the wealthy tended to prefer mansions on large tracts of land. Nonetheless, as the turn of the century approached and urban land became scarcer and costlier in the booming city, a plan emerged to build a row of grand townhouses that would be appealing to those wealthy people who cared less about maintaining huge gardens. The old vacant Cornell Lead Works were demolished in the late 1880s and individual houses began to be constructed. The block was called the Midway because it was halfway between Niagara Square and Forest Lawn Cemetery. A number of architects participated, among them the distinguished firms of Green and Wicks (No. 477) and Marling and Johnson (Nos. 479 and 483). No. 475 at right is the most elaborately ornamented house, displaying Renaissance Revival details.

Above: Ansley Wilcox House (1838), 641 Delaware Avenue, besides possessing an imposing Greek Revival facade, was the place where Theodore Roosevelt was inaugurated as the 26th president of the United States after William McKinley was assassinated while attending the Pan-American Exposition in 1901. In 1838, three companies of the U.S. Artillery established a garrison at this site. The house, with a simpler facade then, was one in a row of officers' quarters. It was a two-family structure that housed both the commanding officer and the post's surgeon. Also, the house faced away from Delaware Avenue and toward the garrison parade grounds. When Poinsett Barracks, as the garrison was called, was vacated in 1845, the house became a private home. It was purchased by Judge Joseph G. Masten who engaged architect Thomas Tilden to add the Greek Revival portico, palladian windows, and stone lintels facing Delaware Avenue. In 1883, Dexter P. Rumsey bought the house and gave it to his daughter and new son-in-law, Ansley Wilcox, as a wedding present. In the library on September 14, 1901, with the Wilcox family and U.S. dignitaries in attendance, Theodore Roosevelt took the oath of office as president of the United States. The house is a National Historic Site.

Twentieth Century Club (1895-1896), 595 Delaware Avenue, was the first club run by women, for women, in the United States. Miss Charlotte Mulligan was a founder and first president of the organization whose purpose was to enrich the cultural and educational environment of its members. The club acquired a brick chapel, formerly the old Delaware Avenue Baptist Church, and when the club's membership and affluence grew sufficiently, they hired E. B. Green to design a proper clubhouse on the chapel site. He renovated the chapel and in front of it built a grand addition that resembles a Venetian palazzo with a heavily rusticated stone base and a refined upper loggia. In his design, Green was probably influenced by several clubs in New York City designed by McKim, Mead & White in the style of Italian Renaissance villas.

Right: Behind the Twentieth Century Club, on the Franklin Street side, there is a cool, shady garden filled with perennials.

The Classic Architecture of Stanford White

The most dazzling architect triumvirate in America in the late 19th and early 20th centuries was that of New York City's Charles Follen McKim, William Rutherford Mead, and Stanford White. The brilliance of McKim, Mead, and White changed the course of American architecture. Of the three talented men, it was the genius of Stanford White (1853-1906) that most importantly influenced the architectural scene in Buffalo.

Stanford White's first contribution to Buffalo architecture was as associate architect to the great H. H. Richardson when he designed the Buffalo Psychiatric Center in 1870. White's second Buffalo work involved the James F. Metcalfe House, designed three years after White had joined McKim and Mead to form their avant-garde architectural firm that attracted the attention of the Metcalfes in Buffalo.

James F. Metcalfe and his widowed mother hired White and his New York City firm in 1882 to design a house for the family. It was built at 125 North Street and stood there until 1980 when the house was demolished to provide a parking lot for the commercial owners of the Williams-Butler mansion next door. The interior of the rambling, informal Metcalfe house was the particular contribution of Stanford White, and his ornamental designs are preserved in Rockwell Hall at Buffalo State College where the original dining room and library have been reinstalled. The hallway and staircase are in the American Wing of the Metropolitan Museum of Art in New York City.

But the tour de force Stanford White buildings in Buffalo are the Williams-Butler and Williams-Pratt mansions — two adjacent great houses for two prominent brothers. Stanford White had an extraordinary gift for domestic architecture, especially residences on a grand scale. His design for banker George L. Williams' house on Delaware Avenue at North Street was as close to palatial as it gets in Buffalo. The opulent Georgian Revival mansion was built between 1895-1898, and George and Annie Williams gave many parties there before selling the house to Edward H. Butler in 1908.

Butler came to Buffalo in 1873 at the age of 23 to start a newspaper in competition with the Commercial, the Courier, and the Express. He founded the Sunday Morning News, which in 1880 became a daily, the Buffalo Evening News, fore-runner of Buffalo's single surviving daily newspaper, the Buffalo News. Butler died in 1914, but his family continued to occupy the house until 1974, so despite its having been built by George Williams, the house is popularly called the Butler Mansion.

The grandest party ever conceived for this ultimate of party mansions was planned by George and Annie Williams and scheduled for the evening of September 6, 1901. The huge guest list included the social and commercial elite of Buffalo and dignitaries from New York State and Washington, D.C. The honored guest was to be U.S. President William McKinley.

The giant crystal chandelier in the entrance hall was lowered from the attic and fitted with new candles ready to illuminate the illustrious guests. Dramatic flower bouquets filled the parlors and dining rooms. Cases of spirits and wines awaited the crowd, and the kitchen bustled with elaborate and sumptuous food preparation.

George L. Williams — Edward H. Butler House (1895-1898), 672 Delaware Avenue, is Buffalo's most impressive mansion still standing today.

At 4:00 p.m. on September 6, President McKinley attended a reception in the Temple of Music at the Pan-American Exposition. He was shaking hands with people in the crowd when a handsome young man with a bandaged hand, Leon Czolgosz from Ohio, came up to the president, pulled out a gun, and shot him twice in the abdomen. The news of the assassination reached the Williams mansion just a couple of hours before the guests were to arrive, and the grandest party ever planned for 672 Delaware Avenue had to be canceled.

George Williams' older brother Charles also hired McKim, Mead, and White in 1895 to design his handsome, red-brick Georgian Revival mansion at 690 Delaware Avenue. Again, Stanford White was the supervising architect, and he created a stately, opulent house fronted with a high curving portico supported by six, two-story Ionic columns, and crowned by an exquisite wrought-iron balustrade. Being somewhat smaller and simpler than 672 Delaware, though nonetheless grand, this house was completed in 1896 while work continued on George's palace until 1898.

Stanford White often designed furniture for the elegant houses he planned. A set of 12 ballroom chairs, which most likely came out of one of his three Buffalo houses, are believed to be the work of Stanford White.

Agnes Ethel, a celebrated actress from Buffalo who knew Stanford White, hired him to design a cemetery monument for her late husband, Francis W. Tracy (1837-1886). White collaborated with his friend, the famous sculptor Augustus Saint Gaudens, to produce the circa 1890 handsome memorial in Forest Lawn Cemetery incorporating a bronze bas-relief sculpture of Tracy by Saint Gaudens.

Stanford White's fame as an architect, which was well deserved, was almost matched by his notoriety as a playboy. On June 25, 1906, White attended a cabaret show on the rooftop theater of Madison Square Garden, which was also one of Stanford White's architectural designs. At a nearby table sat Harry K. Thaw, a 37-year-old millionaire, and his wife, Evelyn, who had been one of White's many mistresses and Thaw knew it. At 11 p.m., Thaw walked to White's table and murdered him with three shots from his pistol.

Above: Carriage house, fountain, and garden at Williams-Butler House.

Right: In the Williams-Butler House, a splendid chandelier, hung from the upper floor, illuminates the entrance hall off which there is a large beamed living room where the walls were originally hung with old Italian brocade above the dark wood of the high wainscoting.

At right is the reception hall of the George L. Williams – Edward H. Butler House (1895-1898), 672 Delaware Avenue. A portion of one of the double parlors is visible in the background. Designed by the renowned New York City architect, Stanford White, the house expresses the grandeur of Georgian Revival style at its most majestic. It was built for George Williams, a highly successful banker, and his wife, Annie, who extravagantly entertained Delaware Avenue society until the house was sold in 1908 to newspaper publisher, Edward H. Butler, and his wife Kate. The Butlers were newcomers to the Delaware Avenue crowd, and when they moved into the house, Butler's colleague, Fingy Connors, indicated what his social progress was likely to be. He said, "Ed, you will find Delaware Avenue is paved with ice the year round." Butler, a native of LeRoy, New York, had arrived in Buffalo as a 23-year-old journalist who started a modest weekly newspaper, the Sunday Morning News, which grew eventually to be today's Buffalo News. Butler's wealth was definitely not old money like most of the rest of Delaware Avenue. But three generations of the Butler family lived in the house for 66 years which would indicate that their money qualified eventually. The entrance to the house off Delaware Avenue is from a porch on the north side of the building, and the grand, formal facade overlooks the garden on the south, or North Street, side.

Following pages: Williams-Pratt House (1895-1896), 690 Delaware Avenue, was designed by Stanford White for Charles H. Williams, older brother of George L. Williams. The Pratt family (Jeannie Pratt being the last to occupy the house for many years) were the final residents of the building before it was adapted for commercial use. It was home to the G.A.R. for a number of years. A particularly interesting feature of the facade is the curved two-story portico supported by six tall Ionic columns and capped by an intricate wrought-iron balustrade. Like its neighbor at 672 Delaware Avenue, the house is opulent Georgian Revival style, though not quite so palatial as its neighbor.

Stephen M. Clement House (1910-1913), 786 Delaware Avenue, built in the period of steel, combines two of the strongest building materials – steel and stone. It is a huge, magnificent mansion with an exterior of rough stone that is trimmed with cut stone and one of E. B. Green's finest residential designs. For inspiration, Green looked back to the English medieval manor house and produced a contemporary dwelling with 25,000 square feet of living space in a style that we call Tudor Revival today. The proliferation of wonderful capped stone chimneys serve a dozen fireplaces. When the last Clement to live in the house, Carolyn Tripp Clement, died in 1941, she gave the house to the American National Red Cross.

Seymour H. Knox, Sr., House (1915-1918),
800 Delaware Avenue, was designed by
Charles Pierrepont H. Gilbert, a New York City
architect famous for all of the mansions he built
on that city's prestigious Fifth Avenue. Knox
was a partner of Frank W. Woolworth in the
vastly successful Woolworth and Knox five-
and-ten-cent stores, a retailing empire with
thousands of outlets. Knox bought the George
Howard mansion, which then sat on the 800
Delaware Avenue site, and all of Knox's friends,
thinking he was planning to move into Howard's
large, stately house, congratulated him on such
a fine upgrade in his living quarters. But Knox
said he had nothing of the sort in mind,
ridiculed Howard's manor, and announced he
was going to tear it down and build a proper
house on the site, and none other than Charles
Pierrepont H. Gilbert was going to design it.
This is what Gilbert produced: a French
Renaissance style limestone mansion with 25
rooms, not including kitchens, pantries, bathrooms, quarters for a large servant staff, cloak
rooms, and walk-in closets. On the eve of
construction in 1915, Knox died and never
saw his dream house.

Right: The ceiling of the music room with
classical decoration inspired by the famous
English architect, Robert Adam.

Following pages: One of the Knox House
parlors and the reception hall.

Above: Campanile Apartments (1929), 925 Delaware Avenue, was one of two large, luxury apartment houses built in Buffalo just before the Depression. The architect of this one was B. Frank Kelly, who came to Buffalo from Canada in 1921 and started a practice here. The Italian Renaissance Revival details are particularly interesting on the upper floors, from eight to twelve. Looking at the massive building, you can easily envision hundreds of apartments inside, but there are only 38. Some have three floors; some come with terraces; one has eight bedrooms with eight-and-a-half baths.

Right: Delaware Avenue Baptist Church (1894-1895), 965 Delaware Avenue, in Richardsonian Romanesque style, is the best work in Buffalo of architect John H. Coxhead. Coxhead (1863-1943) started as an architect in Boston, which was the scene of some of the finest work of Henry Hobson Richardson. Particularly impressive to Coxhead was Richardson's Trinity Church constructed in the middle 1870s. It was Richardson who invented the American Romanesque architectural style that bears his name, and Trinity Church was a prime example of the style. When Coxhead moved to Buffalo in the early 1890s and received the commission to design the Delaware Avenue Baptist Church, he chose Richardsonian Romanesque as the style. Coxhead worked in Buffalo for 30 years before moving to Washington, D.C., to become an architect for the U.S. Army Air Corps.

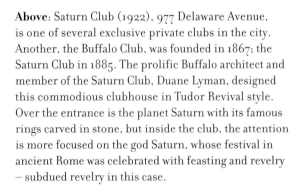

Above: Saturn Club (1922), 977 Delaware Avenue, is one of several exclusive private clubs in the city. Another, the Buffalo Club, was founded in 1867; the Saturn Club in 1885. The prolific Buffalo architect and member of the Saturn Club, Duane Lyman, designed this commodious clubhouse in Tudor Revival style. Over the entrance is the planet Saturn with its famous rings carved in stone, but inside the club, the attention is more focused on the god Saturn, whose festival in ancient Rome was celebrated with feasting and revelry – subdued revelry in this case.

Above: George V. Forman–Oliver Cabana, Jr., House (1892-1893), 824 Delaware Avenue, like nearly all of the great Delaware Avenue houses, is well made and tastefully designed, in this case by E. B. Green. These mansions of the late 19th century present imposing edifices based on centuries-old but much-admired classical design concepts. This venerable house, in Renaissance Revival style has a portico with a traditional gabled entablature supported by two-story columns with embellished Ionic capitals. What is unusual is that those tall circular columns, instead of being made of stone, are constructed of light-colored brick that has been formed in curvilinear shapes.

Right: George F. Rand House (1918-1921) (now, Canisius High School), 1180 Delaware Avenue, was designed by prominent Buffalo architects Franklyn J. and William A. Kidd. George Rand (1867-1919) was president and chairman of the board of directors of Marine Midland, but he was killed in a plane crash near Caterham in Surrey, England before the house was completed. His two sons, however, moved in and lived there for three years before selling it. Canisius High School, which had humble beginnings on Ellicott Street when it was established in 1870, has occupied this elegant Jacobean Revival mansion since 1944. The array of picturesque stone chimneys has separate shafts for each flue, and the shafts are arranged in rows of three.

The entrance gate to Forest Lawn Cemetery (1849), 1411 Delaware Avenue, was designed by the prominent Buffalo architect, George Cary, in 1906. The cemetery is in the National Register of Historic Places.

Right: Forest Lawn Cemetery George K. Birge Monument (1918), 1411 Delaware Avenue, is a classical peristyle in white marble with twelve Doric columns and a sarcophagus resting in the center of the round open platform. Birge was the nationally known manufacturer of wallpapers, as well as president of the Pierce-Arrow Motor Car Company.

Above: Forest Lawn Cemetery Blocher Memorial (1888), 1411 Delaware Avenue, is unquestionably the most lavish tribute to Victorian taste in the cemetery. Young Nelson Blocher fell in love with a family maid, and his parents, aghast at the thought of a marriage beneath their son's station, sent him off to cool his ardor in Italy, where, unfortunately, he became ill and returned home to die. With profound feelings of responsibility for this tragedy, the parents, John and Elizabeth Blocher, conceived an elaborate memorial incorporating their own grieving figures in marble beside their son's dead body with a scantily clothed, voluptuous angel overhead. It is believed that the maid herself posed for the angel sculpture. John Blocher, an industrialist with considerable artistic talent, actually designed the memorial. The marble figures, which took three years to carve, were sculpted from 150 tons of rare Italian Carrara marble by the Swiss-born Italian artist, Frank Torrey. Immense granite stones enclose the sentimental tableau. The upper bell-shaped roof stone, which sits on top of another circular stone, alone weighs 60 tons. The roof rests on giant granite pilasters separated by glass-encased doors. The stone chaise longue on which Nelson lies swings aside to permit access to the burial vaults below.

Above: Forest Lawn Cemetery Francis Walsingham Tracy Monument (circa 1890), 1411 Delaware Avenue, was commissioned by his wife, Agnes Ethel, a celebrated actress, who hired the most famous architect in America at the time, Stanford White, to design it. White, a partner in the New York City architectural firm of McKim, Mead & White, which led a sweeping revival of classical architecture in the late 19th and early 20th centuries, collaborated with an equally famous sculptor, Augustus Saint Gaudens, to produce this handsome memorial incorporating a bronze bas-relief sculpture of Tracy (1837-1886) by Saint Gaudens.

Right: Forest Lawn Cemetery Walden–Myer Mausoleum is a massive neo-Romanesque structure that supports a giant globe, which symbolizes God's sovereignty over heaven and earth. Ebenezer Walden (1777-1857) was an early Buffalo judge and real estate developer, and his son-in-law, Albert James Myer (1829-1880), prognosticated the weather so successfully that he founded the U.S. Weather Bureau. He also became the first commander of the Army Signal Corps. In the foreground is the Samuel Fletcher Pratt memorial.

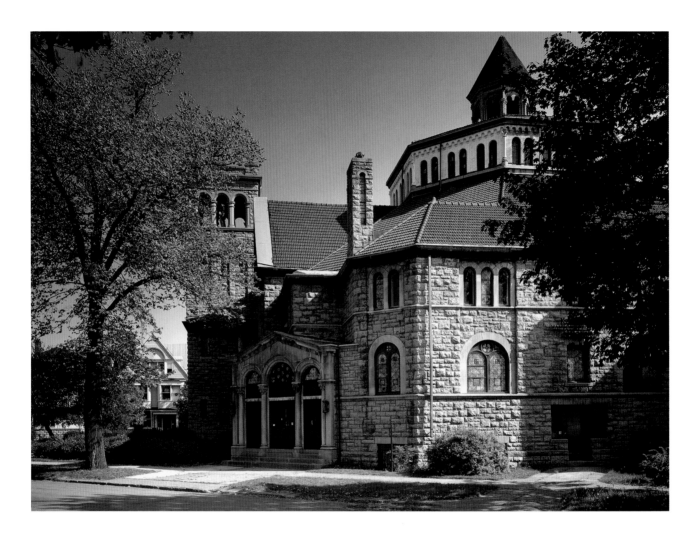

Above: Plymouth Methodist Church (1912), now the Karpeles Manuscript Library Museum, 453 Porter Avenue, was made a city landmark in 1989. The Romanesque style church has two particularly outstanding pictorial stained-glass windows that today filter daylight onto rare and historic manuscripts.

Right: First Presbyterian Church (1889-1891), One Symphony Circle, has a stately, copper-roofed campanile that rises so high it can be seen from nearly any vantage point on the west side of Buffalo. The slender tower, finally completed in 1897, was suggested to the architects, E. B. Green and William S. Wicks, by a similar one in Tournus, France on a 12th-century church. In designing this impressive building, Green and Wicks noted the massive towers that H. H. Richardson had erected for the Buffalo Psychiatric Center at the north end of Richmond Avenue and decided on a soaring tower at the south end of Richmond as well. Further echoing the Psychiatric Center, they also chose Richardsonian Romanesque in Medina sandstone as the style for the exterior of this church. Founded in 1812, First Presbyterian is the oldest religious congregation in Buffalo and had two edifices downtown on Shelton Square before moving north to Symphony Circle.

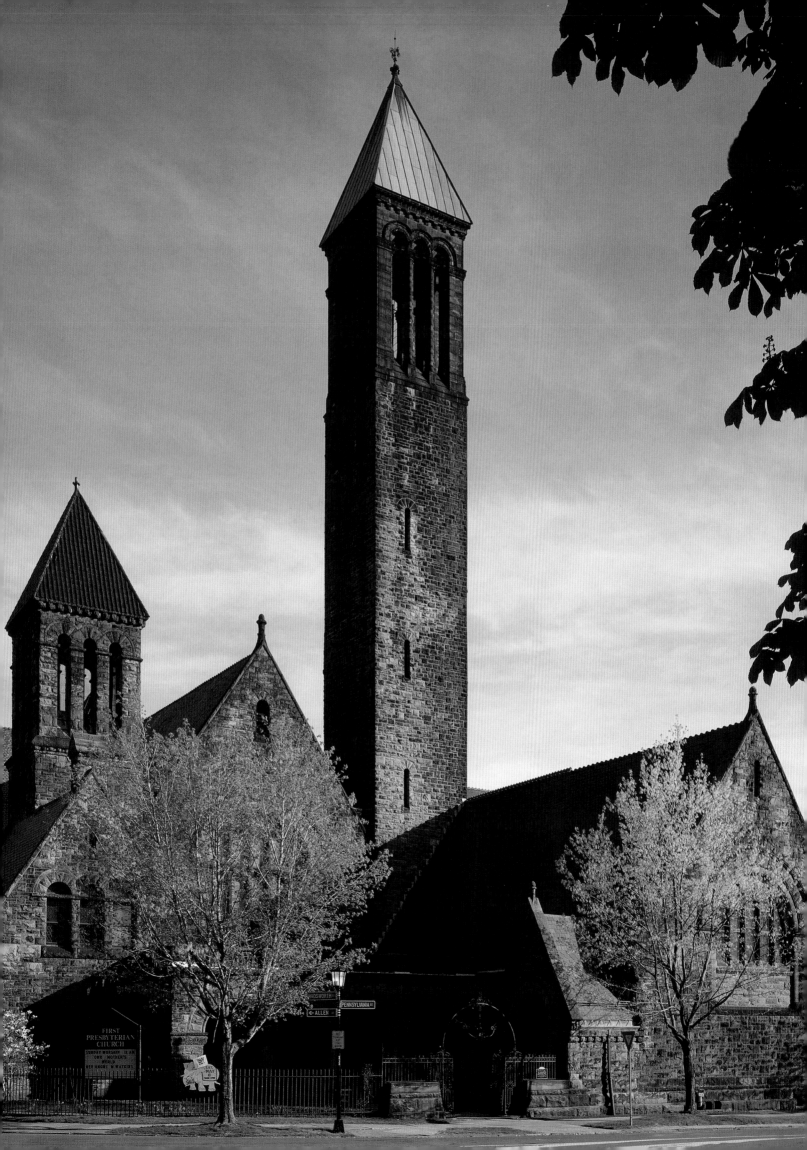

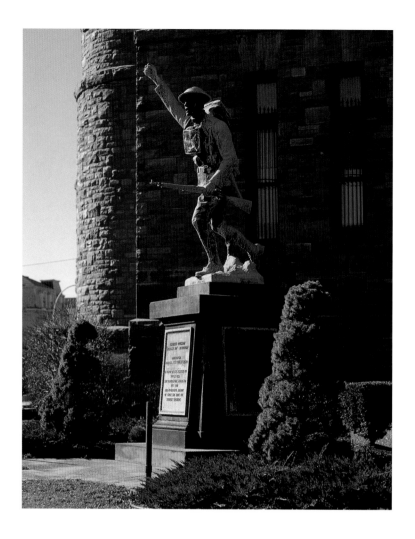

Above: A bronze sculpture of a World War I doughboy stands before the massive Connecticut Street Armory at the corner of Niagara and Connecticut streets.

Preceding pages: Connecticut Street Armory (1898-1900), 184 Connecticut Street, is the second largest armory in New York State and one of the largest in the country. When it opened during the Spanish-American War, it was called the 74th Regiment Armory. William B. Lansing was the architect of this immense, castle-like, Medina sandstone building. The Richardsonian Romanesque style of the structure incorporates towers, crenelated roof lines, tall slit windows, and many other fortress features. The armory is entered through a deeply recessed archway formed by especially large, wedge-shaped stones called voussoirs. Inside, the drill hall was one of the largest truss-spanned, clear-space interiors in the world at the time of construction. Besides superb engineering to provide such breathtaking features, there are handsome carved-oak staircases, doors, and moldings.

Right: St. Louis Roman Catholic Church (1886-1889), 780 Main Street, serves the oldest Catholic congregation in Buffalo. It was started in 1829 on land donated by Stephen LeCouteulx de Chaumont, a Buffalonian of noble French ancestry. Two previous church structures stood on this site before the magnificent current Gothic Revival building was constructed. The present church opened its doors for the first religious service on August 25, 1889: the feast of St. Louis. On the high altar stands a life-size statue of the church's patron, St. Louis IX (1214-1270), king of France, who led the seventh crusade, captured the "true crown of thorns" (enshrining it in a church he built in Paris), and was canonized as a saint. This imposing Main Street edifice was designed by New York City architects, Shickel and Ditmar, who specialized in church architecture. The 245-foot Medina sandstone tower has a 72-foot-tall, pierced-stone spire, the tallest open-work spire ever built completely of stone without reinforcement. The Seth Thomas clock in the tower was a gift from Eldridge G. Spaulding, who lived diagonally across the street. Spaulding was the U.S. Congressman who originated paper currency to finance the Civil War and became known as "the father of the greenback." The church, one of the largest in Buffalo, seats 2,000.

Colonel Francis G. Ward Pumping Station (1909-1915), Porter Avenue at D.A.R. Drive, was named to honor the Buffalo commissioner of public works who led the effort to build it. When constructed, it was the largest pumping plant in the United States. It remains today one of the largest and most completely equipped water treatment and pumping stations in the world. Buffalo's water supply is obtained from an intake 6,000 feet from the pumping station at the head of Niagara River. Treated water from this plant is pumped into 740 miles of distributing mains. Architects for the plant were the capable and versatile firm of Esenwein and Johnson.

In the vast pumping room of the Ward station, there are five giant original steam-driven pumps, each weighing 1,100 tons and standing 60 feet high, taller than many five-story buildings. It is an awesome sight viewed here from an upper balcony. Each of the 1,200-horsepower steam engines has two 30-ton flywheels that drive piston pumps capable of discharging 30 million gallons of water per day through 48-inch pipes. The huge pumps, manufactured by the Holly Pump Company of Lockport, New York, have been replaced by smaller, more powerful electric ones today, so the steam versions stand idle in their splendid majesty surrounded by tile walls and floor and lighted by rows of indoor street lamps.

Left: E. F. Hall House (1900), 467-469 Virginia Street, looking not unlike a house in a medieval French village, is a wonderfully eccentric structure in Chateauesque style – steep-roofed with cresting on the ridge, a round tower with a conical spire on which a fanciful dormer has been attached, and a windowed turret corbeled out from the corner walls, again topped with a spire or candle-snuffer roof as they are often called. Between the first and second floors, there is a wide band that displays various emblems. This real building is more fun than fairy-tale concepts. Hall lived with his family in the No. 467 portion and had his photographic studio in No. 469.

Above: 522 Franklin Street (circa 1850) prominently shows a product that Buffalo was famous for: iron. Not only is the iron on this house highly decorative, it supports a porch that runs the full length of the facade. Iron also furnishes a fence around the shallow front yard.

Above: J. M. Bemis House (1883), 267 North Street, was built for this lumber baron, who accumulated great wealth selling the abundant timber from area forests. He commissioned the architect Joseph Lyman Silsbee (1848-1913) and his junior partner James H. Marling (1857-1895) to design the house. It is pure Silsbee: massive, grand, and grim in Flemish Renaissance style. There are steep tiled roofs, soaring brick chimneys, elaborate terra cotta ornamentation, and two roaring lions crowning the tops of the south and west gables. In recognition of Bemis' source of wealth, the interior is finished in the native woods that made his fortune.

Right: Richard Hatch House (1867), 60 Arlington Place, is a wonderful board-and-batten Gothic Revival structure with an interesting open verge board on the front gable and elaborate carved-wood treatment on the porch. It is a particularly appropriate house for a person of Hatch's profession. He was a stairbuilder.

Above: Duane Lyman House (1948-1950), 78 Oakland Place, is a jewel of a house designed by the distinguished Buffalo architect for his own use. House design in the post World War II era was hardly outstanding, often because good materials and craftsmen were hard to obtain, and houses were often designed without the benefit of architects. But Lyman put both design and construction quality into this attractive house. There is a wonderful fanlight over the entrance and interesting oval windows to either side of it. There is also a side entrance with a small copper-clad roof on wrought-iron brackets. The brick parapet has fenestrations filled with decorative ironwork.

Right: Mayfair Lane townhouses (1928), North Street between Irving Place and Park Street, are Buffalo's first condominiums and created quite a sensation when they were built. E. B. Green and his son, E. B. Green, Jr., were the architects. The lane consists of 20 charming houses facing a flagstone promenade that is elevated above North Street. There is a driveway below the promenade that provides access to garages and servants' quarters. An additional unit, the end house, No. 21, is a small manor approached over a chained drawbridge that is flanked by a Tudor tower. The entrance, below a parapeted wall, is through a medieval arch. This unit was built especially for E. B. Green, Jr., with interior modifications to accommodate the fact that he was disabled and confined to a wheelchair. The lane was designed to look like a street in a historic English hamlet.

800 West Ferry Apartments (1929) was designed by the Buffalo architectural firm of Lawrence Bley and Duane Lyman. Their client was Darwin R. Martin, son of Darwin D. Martin who hired Frank Lloyd Wright to design the house where his namesake son was brought up. In building 800 West Ferry, Darwin R. Martin had the idea that offering two-level luxury apartments with fireplaces, beamed ceilings, and large terraces might appeal to wealthy people who were not particularly attracted to maintaining large single-family estates, yet desiring the luxurious space to which they were accustomed. The Campanile on Delaware Avenue, also built in 1929, offered similar accommodations. At right is the elaborate carved stone entrance of 800 West Ferry.

Above: 17 North Pearl Street (circa 1870) has an ornate Second Empire style entrance with extravagantly embellished double doors. A stairway approaches the entrance from the right side, and an intricately designed wrought-iron railing provides protection on the entry platform.

Right: 135 Linwood Avenue (1911) was the first non-residential building constructed on Linwood Avenue. The prominent Buffalo architect Duane Lyman designed it to be medical offices, although this use didn't fully occur until 1919. The style recalls Greek Revival of almost a century before in America, and the building's facade is reminiscent of that period. In its early years as a medical office building, it was called the "House of Lords," because the doctors who practiced here were all professors at the University of Buffalo's medical school.

Left: Theodore S. Fassett House (circa 1885), 420 Linwood Avenue, on the right makes a dramatic statement on the avenue with its great sloping roof punctured by a massive tower with a candle-snuffer roof, all executed in Queen Anne Shingle style. The interior living spaces offered by this unusual exterior are equally dramatic. To the left of 420, at No. 412, is another equally interesting spacious Queen Anne house.

Above: William H. Scott House (1903), 20 Dorchester Road, was designed by the prolific architectural firm of Green and Wicks. Scott was a builder who was responsible for much of the development of Dorchester Road and other streets of relatively modest houses with 1,500 to 2,000 square feet of living space. He commissioned the firm known in Buffalo for the design of mansions to apply their considerable skills to smaller homes. In 1903, Scott asked Green and Wicks to draw up plans for his own house at 20 Dorchester Road. It sits on a site right at the point where Dorchester curves to meet Bidwell Parkway, and the architects addressed this very visible bend in the road by projecting a two-story turret from the end gable and positioning it to face the curve. It adds to the castle-like effect of this house which has windows with diamond-shaped lead muntins surrounded by decorative half-timberwork.

John T. Howell House (1889), 56 Lexington Avenue, is an impressive Queen Anne style residence with a prominent three-story turret at the left corner. It is easy to imagine the luxurious interior spaces beyond this impressive facade. The irregularity of plan and massing, as well as variety in color and texture, are typical of the Queen Anne style, which borrowed from many classical motifs but combined them in interesting, eccentric ways.

The style, adapted from England, became popular in the United States after the 1876 Philadelphia Centennial Exposition. At that fair, the British government erected two residences for its exposition staff. An American architectural magazine noted that the houses were "the most interesting and by far the most conspicuous and costly buildings erected by any foreign government on the centennial grounds. But the chief thing that will strike the observant eye in this style is its wonderful adaptability to this country, not just to the towns, but to the land at large." The picturesque qualities of Queen Anne electrified Americans who made it one of the most popular residential architecture styles of the late 19th century.

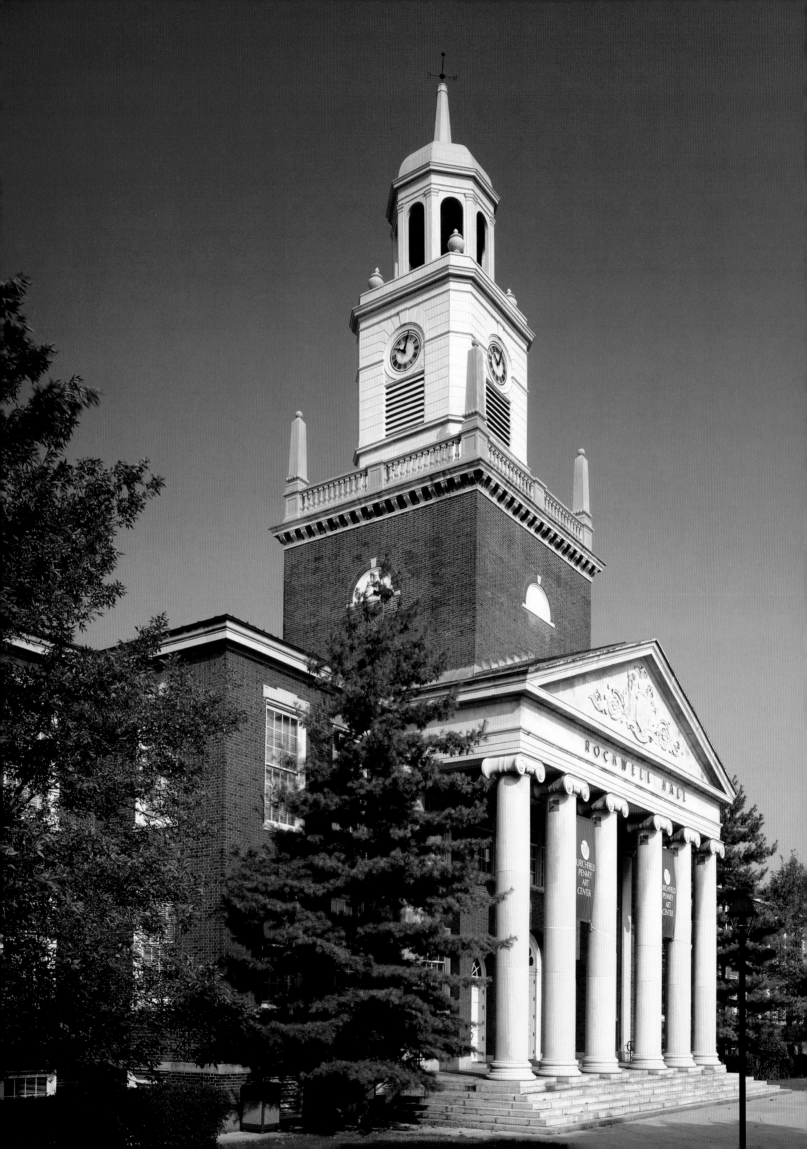

Left: Rockwell Hall (1928), Buffalo State College, 1300 Elmwood Avenue, was designed by William Haugaard, who took inspiration from Independence Hall in Philadelphia. At the time of this building's design, there was also widespread attention being paid to American colonial architecture as a result of the reconstruction of Williamsburg, Virginia. Rockwell Hall contains the Burchfield-Penney Art Center whose art collection includes a large number of paintings by the internationally famous Buffalo artist, Charles Burchfield. The center also houses the Metcalfe Rooms (1882-1884) designed by the renowned New York architect, Stanford White. The Frezalia Metcalfe House stood at 125 North Street until its demolition in 1980, when its interiors were donated to Buffalo State College and the Metropolitan Museum of Art in New York City. The library and dining room with richly carved wood paneling and fireplace mantels were installed in Rockwell Hall.

Above: Buffalo Crematory (1885), 901 West Delavan Avenue, was designed by Edward B. Green when he was 29 years old, just three years after he and his partner William S. Wicks moved their young architectural firm to Buffalo. It is a Richardsonian Romanesque jewel. Still being constructed in Buffalo at the time was H. H. Richardson's monumental Buffalo Psychiatric Center, which may well have inspired Green's superb design for a much smaller scale structure.

Walter P. Cooke House (1915), 155 Summer Street, is a 20th-century adaptation of 16th- and 17th-century English architecture. Cooke was a prominent Buffalo banker and lawyer. Eventually, large old houses like this one surpass in space and maintenance costs the residential desires of most families today. Adaptive use is what saves these great houses. They become institution and corporate headquarters, schools, clubs, social service agencies, commercial offices, and multiple apartments. In this case, the former library is a lawyer's elegant office with ample space to also display a collection of antiques. French doors open to a small but bright conference room.

Following pages: Unitarian Universalist Church (1904), 695 Elmwood Avenue, is an English Gothic style church designed by the talented Buffalo architect Edward Austin Kent. He studied architecture in Paris and practiced in Chicago before coming to Buffalo in the 1880s. Many houses in the city were designed by him, as well as municipal and commercial buildings and this interesting church. He was 58 years old when he was returning home from Europe – aboard the Titanic. His body was recovered and buried in Forest Lawn Cemetery. The inscription on his tombstone reads, "Greater love hath no man than this, that a man lay down his life for his friends."

The most striking feature in the Unitarian Universalist Church is the solid oak hammerbeam ceiling which is stunning in both its design and construction. Buffalo architects, like Edward Kent, made inventive use of the ample timber available in the area in the 19th and early 20th centuries. The interior of this church is considered one of the best Arts and Crafts spaces in the city.

Above: Georgia M. G. Forman House (1928), 77 Oakland Place, was designed by Edward B. Green with stone walls, stone roof, and stone chimneys. There is a Tudor style entrance and you almost expect to see a moat and drawbridge in front of it, but there are, instead, tasteful blends of evergreen and perennial plantings. It is unlikely that E. B. Green put the cross on top of the entrance gable, but it is logical for it to be there since this is currently the residence of the Roman Catholic bishop of Buffalo.

Right: Lafayette High School (1903), 370 Lafayette Avenue, possesses a central tower with a mansard roof that is a neighborhood landmark. It is also listed in the National Register of Historic Places. The school was designed by one of the city's leading architectural firms, Esenwein and Johnson, who employed the French Baroque style for this notable structure. If the tower appears to be rather abruptly cut off, it is. Originally, on top of the mansard roof, there was a cupola supported by a series of columns. The tower had a more finished look then.

H.H. Richardson's Psychiatric Center

The architect H. H. Richardson himself considered the Buffalo Psychiatric Center, then known as the Buffalo State Hospital for the insane, to be his greatest work. The U.S. Department of Interior, which designates national landmarks, agreed and in 1986 made the dramatic structure a National Historic Landmark. Many architectural historians regard Richardson as America's greatest architect, if not of all time at least of the period before Frank Lloyd Wright. So here we have at 400 Forest Avenue in Buffalo, the self-claimed greatest work by one of America's greatest architects.

Henry Hobson Richardson was born in New Orleans in 1838, educated at Harvard University and the Ecole des Beaux Arts in Paris, and began practicing architecture in New York City in 1865. His fame came practically instantaneously.

Richardson's connection to Buffalo occurred through his friend, the renowned landscape architect, Frederick Law Olmsted, who was invited to recommend a park system for Buffalo. One of the civic leaders who brought Olmsted to Buffalo was attorney and politician William E. Dorsheimer, and he was in need of an architect to design his house. Olmsted recommended his New York friend, 30-year-old Richardson. The result was 434-438 Delaware Avenue, built between 1869-1871 in a French style that Richardson had studied while at school in Paris just three years previously.

When Olmsted, in his Buffalo park plan, reserved a large tract of forest on a promontory now bounded by Elmwood and Forest avenues, it was Richardson who was again selected to design the structures to be built on land that Olmsted would landscape. Richardson's Psychiatric Center was designed and built between 1869 and 1880. His plan for the huge complex consisted of a central administration building with curved connecting structures to patient-housing pavilions on either side. The singular, dominating feature of the design was monumental, medieval, double, identical towers, each with four corner turrets and dramatically steep copper roofs mysteriously punctuated with dormered windows, all of which gave the administration building a rather sinister appearance. These great paired towers make the Psychiatric Center one of the most striking public buildings in America.

In 1874, Dorsheimer moved to Albany to become lieutenant governor of New York State. While there, he obtained two more significant architectural commissions for Richardson. One was the state capitol and the other, Albany City Hall.

By the time of his death in 1886 at the age of 47, Richardson had become so famous for his style of Romanesque buildings that the architectural movement he began was named for him: Richardsonian Romanesque.

Buffalo Psychiatric Center (1870-1896), 400 Forest Avenue, is one of the city's most outstanding buildings and was designated a National Historic Landmark in 1986. It was designed by one of America's greatest architects, Henry Hobson Richardson, and is the largest structure he ever designed. It is over 2,000 feet long and contains 400,000 square feet of space. The unusual twin towers, each 185 feet tall, add a portentous quality to the building, especially considering it housed the mentally ill. The brick and red Medina sandstone walls are five feet thick. Andrew Jackson Warner of Rochester was the supervising architect, and the young Stanford White, then on Richardson's staff, was associate architect. The renowned American landscape architect, Frederick Law Olmsted, and his partner Calvert Vaux designed the hospital grounds.

Henry O. Smith House (circa 1930), 33 Tudor Place, presents an imposing mass on a short, block-long street, with a refined, carefully symmetrical Georgian Revival brick facade. The first floor has six-over-nine, double-hung windows; on the second and third levels, they are six-over-six. The central three bays are separated by stone pilasters, which with the parapet and symmetrically placed balustered fenestrations give the facade a simple, but neoclassical appearance. The sheer size of the house bespeaks the generous proportions that were allocated to houses of the 1920s and 1930s.

Following pages: Behind 33 Tudor Place there is a striking formal garden with a lily pond as its focal point.

Seymour H. Knox, Jr., House (1924-1926) was a
wedding present from his mother, who took several
acres of her Delaware Avenue estate and had a grand
house, not unlike her own mansion, constructed on
it. Her house had a side entrance; his had a side
entrance; hers had a ballroom in the basement; his
had a ballroom in the basement, and so on. She had
a flagstone walk constructed between their two
similar houses so that Seymour, Jr., would have an
easy path to join her for breakfast each morning.

Right: The refined interior of the former Seymour
Knox, Jr., House has a grand palladian window
overlooking a marvelous curved staircase with an
elaborate steel-and-brass balustrade.

Above: The formal dining room can be expanded by opening a unique glass wall that is framed and supported by decorative steel and brass. And for large parties, the French windows beyond can be opened to allow guests access to a broad patio that overlooks an expansive garden.

Right: An antique wellhead defines one end of a garden allée at the former estate of Seymour H. Knox, Jr. The 18th-century wellhead has traveled broadly. It was born in Italy, resided in Paris, moved to Hawaii, and settled in Buffalo.

Above: Alexander Main Curtiss House (1895), 780 West Ferry Street, was designed by James A. Johnson two years before he became a partner of August Esenwein to form the architectural firm of Esenwein and Johnson in 1897. Johnson selected Classical Revival as the style for this house with some very fine architectural touches. The semicircular front portico supported by Ionic columns is one of them; the arched entrance door surrounded by a larger arch of leaded-glass windows is another. The house was built by Dr. Alexander Curtiss who practiced medicine in Buffalo for many years. Mrs. Curtiss required her three energetic young sons to use the back stairs rather than the magnificent staircase that is the dramatic central focus of the entrance hall. The four-member Evan Hollister family occupied the house from 1913 until 1922. They required four domestic servants plus a chauffeur to maintain their lifestyle. The house was later occupied by Robert B. Adam, president of Adam, Meldrum & Anderson Company, and his family. It is Buffalo's Ronald McDonald House today.

Right: Chemical No. 5 Firehouse (1895), 166 Cleveland Avenue, is now a private residence. Where once there were fire trucks, vehicle maintenance equipment, and firemen's bunk beds and storage lockers, there are spacious rooms (the living room is 25 by 32 feet) with high ceilings for family living. When this building was erected, fire engines were drawn by horses, so a walled area originally contained stables. It is now a stunning garden. The unusually high steep roof, reminiscent of old Dutch gables, provided interior space where fire hoses were hoisted to dry. Originally, there was a hayloft to store food for the horses. The building was commissioned Engine No. 37; later, it was renamed Chemical No. 5 because of the practice of fighting fires with chemicals including baking soda to increase water pressure. Buffalo's building commissioner at the time the firehouse was built was Philip G. Meyers who said, "Before I retire, I'm going to have one public building put up that will be worth admiring." He instructed the architect, "Anything you want, but make it the best." The architect was Buffalo's Edward Austin Kent who later perished on the Titanic. This is one of the few buildings in Buffalo with some Art Nouveau details.

Thomas J. McKinney House (1927-1929), 35 Lincoln Parkway, was designed by the capable Buffalo architectural firm of Esenwein and Johnson. McKinney inherited a fortune in oil and spent much of it on this incredible house. To build this Renaissance villa, he spent $1 million, which translates to over $10 million today. After his enormous investment, Mr. and Mrs. McKinney lived in the house only four years before being killed in an automobile accident in Orlando, Florida in 1933. At his Lincoln Parkway address, there was garage space for the four Rolls-Royce automobiles that McKinney owned. The house is constructed of Roman brick over poured concrete walls. Today, it is considered to contain some of the foremost wood carving in the United States, possibly exceeded only by Mrs. Horace Dodge's house in Detroit. The woodwork contract alone – executed by the firm of E. M. Hager and Sons, Buffalo wood specialists – came to over $100,000, which is equivalent to more than $1 million today. A crew of 20 expert woodcarvers imported from Germany, Switzerland, and Italy worked two years to accomplish the prodigious effort utilizing rare woods from all over the world.

Above: At the McKinney mansion, the lawn and formal gardens also involved acquiring the best of everything available in the world. For example, the lawn came from the grounds of a Belgian chateau, which contained particularly fine century-old sod that was removed, placed on a freighter, and faithfully watered enroute. Installed beneath the elegant sod was an intricate irrigation system so that Buffalo's summer sunshine would never dry out the historic turf. When neighbors' dogs took a particular fancy to the regal Belgian lawn, McKinney ordered the elaborate ornamental fence and gates of stone, brick, and iron that today continue to surround the property.

Above: A detail of the elaborately carved woodwork. At right, a black walnut lion surmounts the newel post of the main stairway in the McKinney house. To achieve McKinney's stated expectations, E. M. Hager and Sons scoured western New York State and found a living black walnut tree, thick enough for the carving, growing on a farm in Alden. It was purchased at great expense, cut down, and trucked to Buffalo. There, the lion carving was roughly cut from the thickest section of the trunk. This huge block of wood without a single knot was surrounded by sand and inserted in a box that was put in a kiln at 150 F degrees, with a fan constantly circulating fresh air into the box. This curing procedure continued for one year to ensure that the wood would never crack after it was carved. Expert carvers then produced the final carving of a lion which sits 26 inches high, 18 inches deep, and 14 inches wide. The bannister from the hall floor to the first landing is carved from a single piece of black walnut. The carvings are elaborately detailed on both sides of the balustrade and are six inches thick.

Preceding pages: The McKinney library is finished in clear, quarter-sawn English oak. Books are hidden behind elaborately carved bookcase doors with leaded glass depicting the Canterbury Tales. It was reported that Thomas McKinney went to Brentano's Bookstore in New York City and ordered an appropriate library for a gentleman of means, which Brentano's, with their experience and impeccable taste, willingly supplied. Wood in the living room of the McKinney house is hand-carved birch. There are eleven fireplace mantels in the house, all of which were imported from Europe. American walnut was used in the dining room, which has doors carved with heavy garlands of fruit. Hand-carved wood doors and moldings continue throughout the house from the basement to the third floor. There are 24 rooms and 9 bathrooms.

Right: With windows facing east and south, the breakfast room of the Thomas J. McKinney House is flooded with light. The house still contains all of the original chandeliers, sconces, and moldings.

Above: John D. Larkin, Jr., House (1915), 65 Lincoln Parkway, now Buffalo Seminary Larkin House, is a carefully symmetrical Georgian Revival style house with features such as a center entrance punctuated by four classical pilasters over which a trio of windows is similarly separated by pilasters. Above the second floor is a canopy roof and cornice that is surmounted by an additional story with low, horizontal windows. It was designed by the Buffalo architectural firm of McCreary, Wood, and Bradney. Larkin was the son of the founder of the great soap and housewares company. When the elder Larkin died in 1926, John D., Jr., became president of the company and served until 1939 when his brother Harry took over. In 1954, the Buffalo Seminary acquired the house, using it today for receptions and other social functions.

Right: Henry W. Wendt House (circa 1925), 120 Lincoln Parkway – with twin high-pitched gables that on the facade rise above the roof, rough stone, and tall massive chimneys – is representative of Jacobean Revival style, whose inspiration came from English architecture that was popular during the reigns of Elizabeth I and James I, known as the Elizabethan and Jacobean periods. The Wendt brothers, William and Henry, built their Buffalo Forge Company in the heart of Buffalo's German neighborhood to attract Germans to work there. Their industrial pursuits expanded into Wendt Aircraft in the early and middle 1900s. The handsome wrought-iron gate and fence were forged at Armor Welding by Reno Fabrizi.

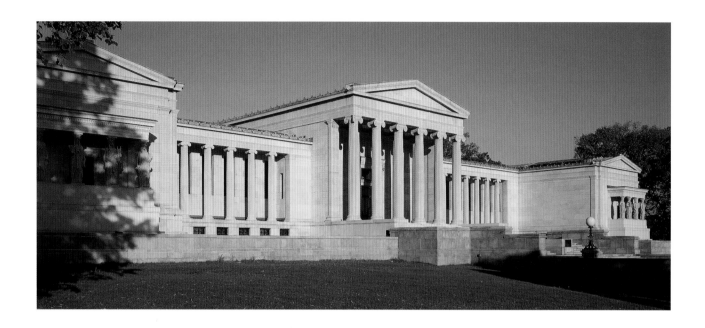

Albright-Knox Art Gallery (1900-1905), 1285 Elmwood Avenue, is Edward Brodhead Green's masterpiece. He designed this massive white marble building in Neoclassical style. It was a gift of the Buffalo industrialist and financier, John J. Albright (1848-1931), who in 1900 wrote the following letter to Guilford Smith, president of the Buffalo Fine Arts Academy: "As a lover of art and a believer in its beneficent influence in such a city as ours, I have long felt that the academy could not fulfill the purposes of its founders and friends without the possession of a permanent and suitable home. Such a home should be exclusively devoted to art, and in its architecture and surroundings should of itself represent the nature of its occupancy. From such inquiries as I have been able to make, I am led to believe that a suitable building would cost from $300,000 to $350,000. This expenditure I am ready to meet." In the end, Albright paid over $1 million to ensure that the building was constructed of the finest quality materials that his friend, the architect E. B. Green, had specified.

Above: Eighteen marble columns stretch across the facade of the Albright-Knox Art Gallery. They have a slightly convex profile suggesting the compression created by supporting massive weight and also to counter the appearance that straight lines seem to sag. Green also spaced the columns not quite an equal distance apart and leaned them ever so slightly toward the center as additional optical compensations. The Greeks did this, too, and Green was always respectful of such design subtleties. The building is in the National Register of Historic Places.

Right: America's preeminent sculptor of the time, Augustus St. Gaudens (1848-1907), was commissioned to carve the caryatids that support the side porches of the Albright-Knox Art Gallery. He was paid $60,000 for eight marble female figures – the largest commission he had ever received and the last one he accomplished before his death.

E.B. Green, Buffalo's Most Prolific Architect

Edward Brodhead Green (1855-1950) was the imaginative architect of numerous distinguished Buffalo buildings. During his long lifetime, Green had a relationship with Buffalo that was so strong that he was very often first among local architects to receive commissions for the design of the city's significant civic, commercial, educational, religious, and residential buildings. The sheer volume of important buildings he produced was remarkable by standards of any architect's output. During a 72-year career, he designed more than 370 major structures from Maine to Indiana with more than two-thirds of them in the city of Buffalo. More than 160 of his Buffalo buildings survive to the delight of local people. The quality and quantity of this architectural legacy becomes readily apparent on the pages of this book.

Green was born in Utica, New York in 1855. He was graduated from Cornell University with a bachelor of architecture degree in 1878. After three years as a junior architect, he and William Sydney Wicks opened an architectural practice in Auburn, New York. They moved to Buffalo in 1881.

When he was 30, Green designed the particularly outstanding Buffalo Crematory (1885), 901 West Delevan Avenue. He built lavish mansions for the rich on Delaware Avenue. Two representative examples are the Charles W. Goodyear House (1903), 888 Delaware Avenue, and the Stephen M. Clement House (1913), 786 Delaware Avenue. The unique condominium development, Mayfair Lane (1928), off North Street, designed in collaboration with his son, Edward B. Green, Jr., has garages and parking on the lower level and a row of Tudor townhouses on the upper terrace level. The end unit masquerades as a miniature castle complete with tower, moat, and drawbridge.

All over the city, his structures display creative applications of many architectural styles. Especially outstanding is his neoclassical Albright Art Gallery (1905). Now called the Albright-Knox Art Gallery, this elegant museum is one of the finest structures in Buffalo with its gleaming stone exterior, Ionic portico, and twin caryatid porches with stone figures sculpted by Augustus Saint Gaudens. The imposing Lockwood Library (1930) on the Main Street campus of the State University of New York at Buffalo represents the joint efforts of Green and his son. Its handsome facade was inspired by the English Renaissance period. The neoclassical Buffalo Savings Bank (1900-1901), now popularly called Goldome, is majestic in size and detail and brings architectural drama to the important downtown intersection of Main and Genesee streets.

In his 95 years, E. B. Green outlived several architect partners – two prolific partnerships being with William S. Wicks and, when Wicks died, his own son, E. B. Green, Jr.

St. Vincent de Paul Roman Catholic Church (1924-1926), 2059 Main Street, now part of the campus of Canisius College, was designed by the Pittsburgh architectural firm of Thomas, Parry, and McMullen. It combines Byzantine and Romanesque styles. The walls of smooth brown sandstone blocks are trimmed with contrasting limestone for a strong visual effect. Rectangular masses create a stair-step effect that leads to the eye-catching dome, which rests on a twelve-sided drum, each side of which has a pair of Romanesque-arched windows. The dome is capped by a Romanesque lantern sheathed in copper. The dome was constructed by the Rafael Guastavino Company of New York City and is unique in western New York State. It is faced with tile in shades of brown and red presenting a particularly striking feature on this urban landscape. The Guastavino Company was renowned for superb tile domes and ceilings constructed by unusual sophisticated techniques. They built the massive vaulted tile ceiling in the main concourse of the 1929 New York Central Terminal, as well as the ceiling vaults in the 1931 Buffalo City Hall.

Left and above: Blessed Trinity Roman Catholic Church (1923-1928), 323 Leroy Avenue, is the work of 30-year-old Chester Oakley (1893-1968) of the architectural firm, Oakley and Schallmo. Remarkably elaborate ornamentation overlays major elements of this church. Terra cotta tiles in myriad colors and depicting countless designs and symbols cover the imposing portal and surround the many other doors. The brickwork on this Romanesque style church is made particularly interesting by including extremely hard-burned bricks, called clinkers, in irregular shapes, which are randomly distributed among the regular red and brown bricks. There's hardly a straight row of bricklaying to be found on the structure – all of which gives the church a medieval look. It is in the National Register of Historic Places.

Following pages: Lockwood Memorial Library (1930-1933), State University of New York at Buffalo, 3435 Main Street, is the focal point of the campus, much as the Rotunda is at Thomas Jefferson's University of Virginia. This elegant building was designed by Edward B. Green in collaboration with his son, E. B. Green, Jr., who was actually credited as architect-in-charge. Father and son were inspired by the approach to classicism of architecture built in the English Renaissance period. Access to this imposing limestone structure is up a long, wide flight of stairs to a massive portico supported by six very tall Ionic columns. Stone balustrades decorate upper portions of the building. The design is particularly lean, but enormously impressive.

Above: Buffalo Museum of Science (1926-1929), 1020 Humboldt Parkway, has a 200-foot-long facade and is 190 feet deep. The long, horizontal building appears to be two stories high and set on a high base, but actually it contains four floors – a high lower floor with three stories over it. Hiding the number of stories on the exterior permitted the architect to simplify the facade and give elegant treatment to tall windows. The first or ground floor contains an auditorium, gift shop, and classrooms. The second floor, entered up a flight of steps from street level, is devoted to exhibit space as is much of the third floor, which also contains offices and the museum library. The fourth floor also has exhibit space and offices, but it further provides access to the Kellogg Observatory (named for the famous Buffalo chemist, Spencer Kellogg) on the roof. This neoclassical structure, with Egyptian style capitals on the entrance columns and griffins decorating the frieze, was designed by the Buffalo architectural firm of Esenwein and Johnson, with James A. Johnson being the principal architect. The total cost of the building exceeded $1 million at a time when the dollar had substantially more value. The museum's parent body is the Buffalo Society of Natural Sciences, founded in 1861.

Claude Bragdon: Unsung Talent Behind the NYS Pavilion

Claude Fayette Bragdon (1866-1946) was a particularly gifted architect with unassailable aesthetic taste and judgment. He championed innovative architecture and was widely considered to be one of the best pen-and-ink artists. Bragdon became one of the most distinguished architects in Rochester, New York.

When he was 24 years old, Bragdon worked briefly for the Buffalo firm of Green and Wicks, who greatly admired his creative talents. During his time there, he met George Cary, another young architect in Buffalo. So when Cary decided to enter the competition for the design of the New York State pavilion (later to become the Buffalo and Erie County Historical Society) at the 1901 Pan-American Exposition, he sought the assistance of this brilliant designer from Rochester.

Their working relationship was revealed in casual letters that Bragdon wrote to relatives in Rochester — excerpts from two of which are reproduced below. The first was written at the Buffalo Club to Bragdon's parents in Rochester on Thursday a.m., April 6, 1900:

> "... I think that I'll stay here over Sunday, so as to have that day too for work. A complete set of plans, a dozen drawings nearly, all of them to be done before next Friday and practically nothing started yet. I made this bargain with Mr. Cary. $10 per day, and in case he wins, this amount to be trebled, i.e. $30 per day. This makes it an objective to see the thing through, and for that reason I've decided to stay into next week though I haven't told him so yet. He pays all my expenses at this club ..."

The second letter was addressed to his sister, May, also in Rochester, and is dated Sunday p.m., April 9, 1900:

> "The competition grows absorbing and I am getting really interested. Yesterday, we (George Cary and Bragdon) drove to the site and decided to change the entire scheme of approaches so as to save some fine old trees, so today we are no farther advanced than we were yesterday, but the improvement is marked. Cary is a good critic, but not very creative. So far we have gotten along splendidly together. ... (Cary) invited me to church today. He pours tea every afternoon at five. ..."

There were only seven submittals to the competition. The Buffalo Park Board liked one; the president of the Historical Society liked another. So the final decision was given to the president of the Architectural League of New York, Robert W. Gibson, who rejected both and selected the Cary/Bragdon proposal. From at least one point of view, Bragdon's drawings were the most beautifully rendered concepts. And as it turned out, he tripled his payment for them.

Buffalo and Erie County Historical Society (1901), 25 Nottingham Court, was built as the New York State pavilion for the 1901 Pan-American Exposition and is the only surviving fairgrounds structure still on its original site—all the others having been intentionally constructed of plaster and demolished when the exposition ended. A competition was held to select an architect for the building. Robert W. Gibson, president of the Architectural League of New York, chose a design by George Cary, a 40-year-old Buffalo architect. He presented a design in the classic order known as Greek Doric, the most distinguished example of which was the Parthenon in Athens. Cary wrote, "The Greek Doric is suggestive of solidity and force, and combines the most subtle and delicate refinement of outlines and proportion that architecture has known." September 5, 1901 was President's Day at the Pan-American Exposition, and President William McKinley along with invited guests attended a luncheon in this building. The next day at a reception in the Temple of Music on the fairgrounds, the president was shot. He died on September 14. In 1987, this handsome marble building was designated a National Historic Landmark. The Buffalo and Erie County Historical Society now housed here was founded in 1862 by an earlier U.S. president, Millard Fillmore, who was also named the organization's first president.

Above and right: Gerard F. Miller House (circa 1920),
now Nichols Middle School, 175 Nottingham Terrace,
is the largest mansion to be built on the former
grounds of the 1901 Pan-American Exposition. Before
that dazzling world's fair occurred, this area was a rural
field north of Scajaquada Creek. During the fair, over
8 million people tramped this 350-acre site. By March
1902, the exposition was in ruins, and the grounds
were gradually prepared for redevelopment. This
imposing stone mansion with Tudor Revival details
was erected two decades later, eventually becoming
too large for single-family use and fortunately finding
adaptive use as a prestigious private school.

Following pages: Louis Surdam House (1928-1930),
62 Middlesex Road, presents a handsome symmetrical
facade with windows in each bay aligned vertically
through three stories. A slate mansard roof on the
third floor lends the house a French style connection.
The first two stories of this solid house are built of
stone and stucco. Surdam chose these building materials
despite the fact that he ran a company, Osmose, that
treated lumber. The prominent Buffalo architect,
Duane Lyman, designed the house. The L-shaped
structure contains 7,300 square feet of living space.

Preceding pages: Darwin D. Martin House (1904-1906), 125 Jewett Parkway, is a masterpiece from America's greatest architect, Frank Lloyd Wright (1867-1959). Wright designed more than 1,000 buildings that were built in 40 states, Canada, and Japan. Carla Lind, a Wright scholar, said, "If you were going to save the top 10 percent of Wright's buildings, the Darwin Martin House would clearly be among them." Dr. Frank Kowsky, New York State Preservation Board, added, "The Martin house is the most important piece of domestic architecture in New York State." Our nation also recognized the importance of this residence by designating it a National Historic Landmark in 1986. Wright was 35 years old when he designed the Martin house, one of the largest and most complex of his Prairie style buildings. It has an open plan allowing a free flow of space between rooms and from the interior to the exterior. In the 10,000-square-foot house, there is a 70-foot-long room that serves as library, living, and dining areas. Because he was given an unlimited budget, Wright designed the furniture, including the first version of his famous barrel chair.

Above: Graycliff (1927), 6472 Old Lakeshore Road, Derby, was the Darwin D. Martin summer house on the shore of Lake Erie. The architect was Frank Lloyd Wright. The failing health of Martin's wife, Isabelle, precluded their annual summer trip to Lake Placid, so they decided to build this summer house in nearby Derby. Isabelle, whose eyesight was impaired, was not happy with the house that Wright had designed for them at 125 Jewett Parkway. It was too dark for her to see things in it, she maintained. So when they planned this summer retreat, Martin put Isabelle in charge of working with Frank Lloyd Wright to get things right this time. Wright, usually adamant about having his way, was particularly receptive to the requests of his new client. The windows are more generous than usual for Wright, thereby accommodating Isabelle's desire for more light; they also supplied enhanced lake breezes to partially emulate Adirondack air. Windows on both floors are designed to capture and direct cooling breezes. In the living room, windows extend from floor to ceiling on both sides of the room. Darwin Martin's bedroom is on the opposite side of the long house from Isabelle's. Any closer and his snoring would have kept her awake, she said. Isabelle much preferred this summer house to her grand mansion in the city. Even Wright liked what he had created and used this house as his model for world-famous Falling Water near Pittsburgh.

The Man Who Brought Frank Lloyd Wright to Buffalo

The person singularly responsible for all of the Frank Lloyd Wright structures found in Buffalo is Darwin D. Martin (1865-1935), who was secretary of the Larkin Company, a large mail-order soap and housewares firm in the city. Martin, along with Elbert Hubbard, another top executive in the company (later of Roycroft fame), and John D. Larkin, president, conceived many innovative ideas to stimulate sales by offering an endless variety of premiums. Martin, who started to work for Larkin's company at the age of 14, became a particularly effective and valued executive in the company. His innovative efforts included the invention of a card-file system that revolutionized accounting procedures not only at the firm but throughout American industry.

The immense success of the Larkin Company led to the need for a new administration building at the turn of the century. During Christmas 1900, Martin visited his brother in Oak Park, Illinois, who took him to see Frank Lloyd Wright's home that Wright had designed for himself. Martin was instantly impressed with Wright's work and became an enthusiastic life-long supporter.

In 1901, Martin persuaded Larkin to commission Wright to design the new office building that the company needed. It was truly an advanced office building, incorporating many innovative features, such as central air conditioning. Unfortunately, the magnificent structure, which would today adapt easily for many uses, was demolished in 1950.

Martin also hired Wright to create a fabulous residence for his own family on land he purchased along Jewett Parkway. That project led to two additional Wright-designed houses on Martin's land: the charming gardener's cottage and the George Barton House for Martin's sister, Delta, and her husband. The Jewett Parkway complex also originally included a greenhouse, two-story garage and stable, and a conservatory connected to the main house by a long pergola.

Martin's enthusiastic initiative inspired a fellow executive at Larkin, William R. Heath, to have Wright design a house on Soldiers Place for him and his wife, Mary, who was the sister of Elbert Hubbard and Mrs. John D. Larkin. Still another Larkin Company top manager, Walter V. Davidson, decided to have a home at 57 Tillinghast Place done by Wright in 1908. Completing Wright's architectural contributions to the Buffalo landscape was the summer house, Graycliff, that he designed for Darwin Martin at Derby on the south shore of Lake Erie in 1927.

If events had turned out differently, there would be a final Frank Lloyd Wright structure in Buffalo today. Darwin Martin commissioned Wright to design an appropriate monument for a family lot that Martin had purchased in Section H of Forest Lawn Cemetery. Wright created a flight of shallow stone steps, under each one of which was an individual burial crypt, leading to a tall family monument at the crest of the gradual slope of the lot.

Martin was delighted with the design, but thinking it would be expensive and not a sound investment, nicknamed it "The Martin Blue Sky Mausoleum." Martin probably would have been happy to pay the cost of constructing the terraced memorial, but the plans were completed just weeks before the 1929 stock market crash, and Martin's fortunes evaporated shortly thereafter, so neither he nor any member of his family buried in the lot today has any marker whatsoever. It is also unfortunate that the only cemetery monument that Frank Lloyd Wright designed was never built.

Above: William R. Heath House (1904-1905), 76 Soldiers Place, was also designed by Frank Lloyd Wright. Heath was a vice-president at the Larkin Company and was introduced to Wright by fellow Larkin executive, Darwin D. Martin. Heath had purchased a long, narrow lot at Soldiers Place along Bird Avenue. The lot presented a serious problem for Wright in trying to fit a substantial Prairie-style house that normally required wide outdoor spaces. He placed the house close to the sidewalk on the Bird Avenue side and then, to provide privacy, raised floor and window levels to limit pedestrian view of the interior. This placement also permitted a private garden to the rear of the house. Privacy was further enhanced by careful positioning of a broad chimney, stained-glass windows, and an unusually small entrance. The architectural historian Henry-Russell Hitchcock wrote,"Despite their low spreading quality, Wright's houses are monumental, and for all their simplicity, the clear interlocking of parts produces compositions of great interest and variety."

Right: Gardener's Cottage (1905), 285 Woodward Avenue, was an integral part of the Darwin D. Martin estate complex. Originally, there were six buildings on the estate: the main house, the George Barton House (built for Martin's sister, Delta, and her husband), the gardener's cottage, a two-story garage and stable, a greenhouse, and a conservatory connected to the main house by a long pergola. This was where Frank Lloyld Wright's Prairie style reached its fullest expression. The gardener of this wood-and-stucco cottage was Reuben Polder, who had to provide fresh flowers daily for every room in the main house, a task which he assiduously accomplished until his employer died in 1935.

Following pages: The dining room of the Gardener's Cottage.

Left: As is evident in this interior view of the
Gardener's Cottage on the Darwin D. Martin estate,
the gardener, Reuben Polder, lived very well indeed.
This view looks from the kitchen into the living room.

Above: George Barton House (1903-1904), 118
Summit Avenue, was the first of Frank Lloyd Wright's
Buffalo buildings to be completed. Its low profile
reflects the expansiveness of the American prairie.
Wright's use of unadorned natural materials – brick,
concrete, and oak – reflected an organic approach.
George Barton worked for the Larkin Company and
was married to Darwin Martin's sister, Delta. Brendan
Gill wrote a biography of Frank Lloyd Wright in which
he stated, "The Barton house is a small and nearly
perfect jewel, a shelter cozy and yet filled with light,
and most people who visit both houses are apt to
prefer it to the Martin house."

Walter V. Davidson House (1908), 57 Tillinghast Place, was designed by Frank Lloyd Wright for another Larkin Company executive. Most ceilings in Wright houses are relatively low, but in this residence, Wright made the living room two stories high. To add to the room's spaciousness and light, he added a huge, two-story bay window at one end and clerestory windows along the north and south walls. Wright liked low or flat roofs and skylights, which often leaked. From one of Wright's buildings at Florida Southern College, President Ludd Spivey wrote, "The skylight keeps leaking and I have water all over my desk. What should I do?" Wright wrote back, "I guess you are going to have to move your desk." At the Tulsa home for Wright's cousin, Richard Lloyd Jones, the flat roof leaked in a rainstorm, and Mrs. Jones commented, "That's what happens when you leave a work of art out in the rain." Davidson, fortunately, had no such problems.

Right: Unusual for Frank Lloyd Wright, he designed a two-story, cathedral-ceiling living room for the Davidsons. To enhance the room's light even further, he created a two-story bay window at one end of the room. The furniture, also, was designed by Wright.

South Buffalo

Joseph Dart's Grain Elevator

When Buffalo became the western terminus of the Erie Canal, the city grew to be the busiest grain-transfer port in the world, surpassing London, Odessa, and Rotterdam. The relatively small Erie Canal boats had no sails or keels to navigate the Great Lakes, and even the smallest lake ships could not traverse the narrow, shallow canal. So all cargo had to be unloaded, stored, and reloaded in Buffalo. Before Joseph Dart's elevator, low-paid Irish shovelers jumped into the hold of the lake cargo ships and shoveled wheat into baskets, which were then carried on the backs of more Irish stevedores to warehouses. Despite the cheap labor, it was a slow, back-breaking process.

In 1842, Dart conceived a new approach. He attached buckets to a vertical belt and powered it by a steam engine. The buckets reached down into the wheat in the hold of a ship, scooped up the grain and dropped it into tall warehouses called grain elevators. His first invention unloaded 2,000 bushels of grain an hour. By 1855, he had 10 grain towers with a storage capacity of 1.5 million bushels and elevators that could unload 22,400 bushels of grain an hour from lake ships.

Today, the grain elevators in Buffalo constitute the most outstanding collection of extant elevators in the U.S. Fifteen of them still stand on Buffalo's waterfront. The Great Northern elevator is the oldest remaining one, having been built in 1897. It is also the only surviving metal elevator; all of the others in existence are made of concrete. Concrete Central became one of the largest grain unloading and transfer facilities in the world after it was completed in 1914.

Besides its collection of storage elevators, Buffalo is still the largest grain-milling center in the country. Wheaties and Cheerios are made at the cereal plant of the General Mills facility, which includes grain silos, a flour mill, and the cereal plant. Con Agra, Inc., besides operating a grain elevator, makes bulk flour for bakeries in eastern U.S. ADM Milling Company also receives and stores grain, and, as its company name implies, operates a mill.

Early grain elevators were made of wood and later involved metal, but their capacity was limited. Finally, concrete elevators reinforced with steel were constructed that could store seven million bushels, which is 210,000 tons of grain. Elevators like these stand 250 feet high like 25-story skyscrapers.

Building reinforced concrete elevators was a complex, exacting process. A gigantic, steel-and-wood form of curvilinear shape about four feet high was built and placed on the foundation slab. Concrete was poured into this slipform on a continuous basis until the entire height of the elevator was reached. Workers operated screw jacks to raise the slipform six inches an hour. This allowed the concrete at the bottom of the form to set sufficiently so that it maintained its shape, yet meant that the concrete at the upper part of the form was still sufficiently wet so that the next concrete pour would bond with it.

Concrete had to be poured continuously, 24 hours a day, for several weeks. Each jack man had twelve jacks to attend to, and a whistle sounded to raise each jack one turn. Raising a slipform six inches required 24 whistle signals an hour. In that hour, a jack man would make 288 turns, close to five a minute, on each of his twelve jacks. There was never a minute's rest, and if the jack man missed turns, his section of the slipform would be lower and cause dangerous stress on the huge form.

Reinforcing steel was laid as the concrete was poured, and this, too, had to be a precisely timed effort. A carefully measured quantity of steel was delivered to the jobsite at the beginning of construction. If a considerable amount of steel was left over at the end of the job, it meant that the elevator had not been sufficiently reinforced. Although there were reports of unused steel being dumped in the Buffalo River to cover construction omissions, no concrete elevator in Buffalo has collapsed from weakness. Grain dust, however, can explode violently as it did at the Husted elevator in 1913 killing 33 people and injuring 80 others.

Page 163: Great Northern Grain Elevator (1898), Ganson Street, is a monumental brick structure that provides weather protection for the system of steel bins inside. From the middle 1800s to the middle 1900s, the banks of the Buffalo River in South Buffalo were crowded with grain elevators, flour mills, and iron foundries. This one, variously known as the Mutual Elevator and the Pillsbury Elevator, was designed by engineer Max Toltz and architect D. A. Robinson. It was built by James Stewart & Company.

Above and left: South Park Conservatory (1898), South Park Boulevard at McKinley Parkway, was designed by Lord and Burnham Company. When the Crystal Palace was erected in London in 1851 of prefabricated iron structural framework and glass panels, it inspired greenhouse manufacturers like Lord and Burnham to adopt the technology and mass produce them. The South Park Conservatory was built as a focal point in the last of the parks designed for Buffalo by Frederick Law Olmsted. At the time it was built, this conservatory was the third largest in the U.S. and the ninth largest in the world. It contains 15 greenhouses today with 1,500 varieties of plants and attracts more than 100,000 visitors annually.

Our Lady of Victory Basilica (1922-1926), Ridge Road at South Park Avenue, Lackawanna, is a spectacular church that was the vision and accomplishment of an extraordinary Roman Catholic priest, Father Nelson Baker. At age 34, Baker left a successful grain and feed business to become a priest. He devoted his priestly service to the Blessed Virgin Mary, Our Lady of Victory, and turned around a failing parish in Lackawanna, expanding its humanitarian services, including an infant home and a maternity hospital for unwed mothers. He housed, fed, and educated tens of thousands of orphaned and troubled boys. After 60 years of charitable work, he crowned his priesthood with this magnificent shrine honoring his spiritual companion during all those years. The exterior of this ornate building is clad in Italian Carrara and Georgia marble. The twin towers are 165 feet high. The multiple domed roofs are copper as are the 18-foot-high, trumpet-blowing angels at the four corners of the dome.

Right: The great dome of Our Lady of Victory Basilica, with a diameter of 80 feet and a height of 113 feet, is among the largest in the country.

Twisted red Baroque columns of rare Pyrenese marble support a frame around a pure white marble, nine-foot statue of Our Lady of Victory, the focal point of the ornate main altar.

Previous pages: The original pipe organ in the nave was a custom-made Wurlitzer manufactured in North Tonawanda. It was replaced in 1981 with a Delaware organ, also made in North Tonawanda.

Left: The 14 Stations of the Cross, each beautifully carved life-size from a single block of Italian marble, line the aisles leading to side altars.

Above: The east portico in the background is topped with marble sculptures of 30 young girls and a nun under the guardianship of an angel. It is a tribute to the Sisters of St. Joseph who have cared for homeless parish children since 1856. Above the west portico of Our Lady of Victory Basilica and carved in stone are a cluster of 30 small boys surrounding Father Baker – an image ordered in his likeness by his assistants as a surprise.

"There are a thousand angels in the basilica," Father Baker said. "Everywhere you look, an angel looks back." There are 46 varieties of marble from around the world and more than 150 works in stained glass. Solid bronze doors are everywhere, even in back hallways. The interior is filled with gold leaf, stenciling, and stone statuary.

Index

135 Linwood Avenue 100, 101
17 North Pearl Street 100
412 Linwood Avenue 102, 103
522 Franklin Street 93
800 West Ferry Apartments 18, 98, 99
Adam, Meldrum & Anderson Company 124
Adam, Robert B. 70, 124
Adler, Dankmar 22
ADM Milling Company 162
Aiken, William M. 32
Albany City Hall 114
Albright Art Gallery 16, 17, 138
Albright Art School 17
Albright, John J. 15, 136
Albright–Knox Art Gallery 13, 136, 137, 138
American Glucose Company 14
American Institute of Architects 32, 34
American National Red Cross 68
Ansonia Building 38
Apple, R. W. 13
Architectural League of New York 145
Armor Welding 134
Asbury United Methodist Church 29
Atwood, Charles B. 40
Babcock Electric automobile 17
Baker, Father Nelson 166, 171
Barton, George, House 153, 154, 159
Bell Aircraft Company 17
Bemis, J. M., House 94
Bethlehem Steel Company 17, 19, 20
Bethune, Louise Blanchard 34
Bethune, Robert 34
Birge, George K., Monument (Forest Lawn) 80, 81
Blessed Trinity Roman Catholic Church 140, 141
Bley, Lawrence 98
Blocher Memorial (Forest Lawn) 82
Blocher, Elizabeth 82
Blocher, John 82
Blocher, Nelson 82
Bossom, Alfred 34
Bragdon, Claude Fayette 144
Breuer, Marcel 21
Buffalo and Erie County Historical Society 13, 16, 144, 145
Buffalo Bisons 21
Buffalo City Courthouse 21
Buffalo City Hall 2–4, 6, 8, 18, 19, 138
Buffalo Club 48, 50, 51, 78, 144
Buffalo Crematory 107, 138
Buffalo Fine Arts Academy 136
Buffalo Forge Company 134
Buffalo Lighthouse 14
Buffalo Museum of Science 18, 38, 141
Buffalo News 60
Buffalo Park Board 144
Buffalo Psychiatric Center 60, 84, 107, 114, 115
Buffalo pumping station 38, 90, 91
Buffalo Savings Bank 42, 43, 138
Buffalo Seminary Larkin House 134
Buffalo Society of Artists 17
Buffalo Society of Natural Sciences 141
Buffalo State College 60, 106, 107
Buffalo State Hospital 114, 115
Burchfield, Charles 107
Burchfield–Penney Art Center 13, 107
Burlington Arcade (London) 42
Burnham, Daniel 40
Butler, Edward H. 60, 64
Butler, Kate 64

Calumet Building 38
Campanile Apartments 18, 76, 98
Canisius College 138
Canisius High School 78, 79
Carlisle, Henry G. 32
Cary, George 80, 144
Caulkins, Franklin W. 34
Cazenovia Park 14
Centerpointe 20, 21
Chemical No. 5 Firehouse 124, 125
Chicago Columbian Exposition 40, 42
Ciminelli Development Company 20, 21
City Courthouse 21
City Hall 2–4, 6, 8, 18, 19, 138
Clark, Donald 21
Clement, Carolyn Tripp 68
Clement, Stephen M., House 68, 69, 138
Cleveland, President Grover 48
Colonel Francis G. Ward Pumping Station 38, 90, 91
Con Agra, Inc. 162
Concrete Central grain elevator 16, 162
Connecticut Street Armory 86–88
Connors, Fingy 64
Cooke, Walter P., House 108, 109
Cornell Lead Works 56
Coxhead, John H. 76
Crystal Palace (London) 165
Curtiss, Alexander Main, House 38, 124
Curtiss, Dr. Alexander 124
Curtiss-Wright Aircraft Company 17
Czolgosz, Leon (assassin) 62
D. H. Burnham & Company 40
Dart, Joseph 13, 162
Darwin D. Martin House 150, 151, 152
Davidson, Walter V. 153
Davidson, Walter V., House 160, 161
de Chaumont, Stephen LeCouteulx 88
Delaware Avenue Baptist Church 58, 76, 77
Delaware Park 14
Delaware pipe organ 171
Dennis Building 36
Dodge, Mrs. Horace 126
Dorsheimer, William E. 114
Dorsheimer, William E., House 52
Duerr, Edward, House 18
Dun and Bradstreet 36
Dun Building 15, 36, 37
E. M. Hager and Sons (wood specialists) 126, 128
E. R. Thomas Motor Company 17
Ellicott Square Building 15, 38, 40, 41
Ellicott, Joseph 40
Erie Canal 13, 14, 20, 162
Erie County Community College 30, 31, 32
Erie County Savings Bank 21, 48
Esenwein and Johnson Architects 38, 40, 90, 110, 126, 141
Esenwein, August Carl 38, 124
Ethel, Agnes (actress) 62, 82
Exposition Universale (Paris) 48
Fabrizi, Reno 134
Fairfield Branch Library 15
Falling Water House (Pittsburgh) 152
Fassett, Theodore S., House 102, 103
Fillmore, President Millard 13, 34, 48, 52, 145
First Presbyterian Church 84, 85
First Unitarian Church 34
Forest Lawn Cemetery 13, 16, 56, 62, 80, 110, 153
Forest Lawn Cemetery Delaware Avenue gate 80

Forman, George V.–Cabana, Oliver, Jr., House 78
Forman, Georgia M. G., House 110
Franzen, Ulrich 21
G.A.R. 64
Gardener's Cottage 154–158, 159
General Electric Company 38
General Electric Tower 38, 39
General Mills grain silo, flour mill, cereal plant 162
George B. Post & Sons Architects 52
George Barton House 153, 154, 159
Gibson, Robert W. 32, 144, 145
Gilbert, Charles Pierrepont H. 70
Gill, Brendan 159
Gilman, Arthur 48
Goldman, Mark 18
Goldome 43, 138
Goldstein, Eli 18
Goodyear family 18
Goodyear, Charles W., House 138
grain elevators 12, 13, 162, 163
Graycliff 152, 153
Great Northern grain elevator 162, 163, 165
Green and Wicks 56, 103, 144
Green, Edward. B. Jr. 96, 138, 141
Green, Edward Brodhead 36, 42, 58, 68, 78, 84, 96, 107, 110, 136, 138, 141
Grosvenor Library 13
Guaranty Building 15, 22–27
Guaranty Construction Company 24
Hall, E. F., House 92, 93
Hamlin, Cicero 14
Harrison and Abramovitz Architects 20
Hatch, Richard, House 94, 95
Haugaard, William 107
Heath, Mary 153
Heath, William R. 153
Heath, William R., House 154
Hitchcock, Henry-Russell 154
Holland Land Company 40
Hollister, Evan 124
Holly Pump Company 90
Hooker Chemical Company 20
Houston, Frederic K. 21
Howard, George 70
Howell, John T., House 104, 105
Hoyt, William 15
HSBC Center 21
Hubbard, Elbert 153
Husted grain elevator 162
Huxtable, Ada Louise 5
Illuminating Gas Company 29
Independence Hall (Philadelphia) 107
James Stewart & Company 165
Jefferson, Thomas 141
Jewett family 18
Jewett House 38
Johnson, James Addison 38, 40, 124, 141
Jones, Richard Lloyd 160
Karpeles Manuscript Library Museum 84
Kellogg, Spencer 141
Kelly, B. Frank 76
Kensington automobile 17
Kent, Edward Austin 45, 110, 124
Kidd, Franklyn J. 78
Kidd, William A. 78
Kleinhans Music Hall 18, 19
Knox family 18
Knox, Seymour H., Jr., House 120–123
Knox, Seymour H., Sr., House 70–75

Kowsky, Dr. Frank (NYS Preservation Board) 152
Lackawanna Steel Company 15, 17
LaFarge, John 48
Lafayette High School 38, 110, 111
Lafayette Hotel 34
Lansing, William B. 88
Larkin Company 15, 153, 154, 159
Larkin, Harry 134
Larkin, John D. 15, 153
Larkin, John D. Jr., House 134
Liberty Building 34, 35
Lincoln, President Abraham 34
Lind, Carla 152
Lockwood Memorial Library 138, 141–143
Lord and Burnham Company 165
Lyman, Duane 78, 98, 100, 146
Lyman, Duane, House 96
M&T Plaza 21
Manufacturers and Traders Trust Company 21
Marine Midland Bank 78
Market Arcade 42
Marling and Johnson Architects 56
Marling, James H. 94
Marshall, G. B. 42
Martin Blue Sky Mausoleum 153
Martin, Darwin D. 15, 98, 152–154, 159
Martin, Darwin D., House 16, 150–152
Martin, Darwin R. 98
Martin, Delta 153, 154, 159
Martin, Isabelle 152
Masten, Judge Joseph G. 56
Mayfair Lane townhouses 96, 97, 138
McCreary, Wood, and Bradney Architects 134
McKim, Charles Follen 60
McKim, Mead & White Architects 38, 58, 82
McKinley, President William 16, 38, 48, 56,
   60, 62, 145
McKinney, Thomas J. 126, 132
McKinney, Thomas J., House 38, 126–133
Mead, William Rutherford 60
Metcalfe Rooms 107
Metcalfe, Frezalia, House 107
Metcalfe, James F. 60
Metcalfe, James F., House 60
Metropolitan Museum of Art (New York) 60, 107
Meyers, Philip G. 124
Midway 54–57
Milburn, John 15
Miller, Gerard F., House 146, 147
Mulligan, Charlotte 58
Museum of Science 18, 38, 141
Mutual grain elevator 163
Myer, Albert James 82
National Aniline and Chemical Company 15
New York Central Terminal 138
New York State Capitol 114
New York State pavilion 144, 145
Niagara Hudson Power Company 15
Niagara Mohawk Building 38, 39, 176
Nichols Middle School 146, 147
O'Rourke, Jeremiah 32
Oakley and Schallmo Architects 141
Oakley, Chester 141
Old County Hall 14, 28, 29
Old Post Office 30–32
Olmsted, Frederick Law 14, 52, 114, 165
Our Lady of Victory Basilica 166–171
Pan-American Exposition 16, 18, 38, 48, 56,
   62, 144–146

Parthenon (Athens) 145
Pei, I. M. 21
Philadelphia Centennial Exposition 104
Pierce-Arrow automobile 17
Pierce-Arrow Motor Car Company 18, 80
Pillsbury grain elevator 163
Plymouth Methodist Church 84
Poinsett Barracks 56
Polder, Reuben (Darwin Martin's gardener)
   154, 159
Porter, Cyrus K. 48
Post, George B. 52
Pratt, Jeannie 64
Pratt, Pascal 52
Pratt, Samuel Fletcher, Memorial 82, 83
Prudential Building 24–27
Prudential Insurance Company 24
pumping station 38, 90, 91
R. G. Dun Company 36
Rafael Guastavino Company 138
Rand family 18
Rand, George F. 78
Rand, George F., House 78, 79
Rapp, Cornelius W. 45
Rapp, George W. 45
Rath Building 21
Rathbun, Benjamin 13, 34
Republic Steel Company 15, 17, 19
Richardson, Henry Hobson 13, 21, 52, 60, 76,
   84, 107, 114
River Mist 21
Riverside Park 14
Robinson, D. A. 165
Rockwell Hall (Buffalo State College) 60, 106,
   107
Ronald McDonald House 124
Roosevelt, President Franklin 48
Roosevelt, President Theodore 56
Root, Delia L. 45
Roycroft 153
Rumsey family 18
Rumsey, Dexter P. 56
Saarinen, Eero 19
Saarinen, Eliel 19
Saint Gaudens, Augustus 62, 82, 136, 138
Saturn Club 78
Schoellkopf family 18
Schoellkopf, Jacob F. 15
Schoellkopf, Jacob F. II 15
Scott, William H., House 103
Selkirk, John H. 29
Shahn, Ben 20
Shea's Buffalo Theatre 17
Shea's Center for the Performing Arts, 44–47
Shea, Michael 45
Shickel and Ditmar Architects 88
Silsbee, Joseph Lyman 94
Sisters of St. Joseph 171
Smith, Guilford 136
Smith, Henry O., House 116–119
South Park 14
South Park Conservatory 164, 165
Spaulding, Eldridge G. 88
Spivey, Ludd 160
St. Louis IX, king of France 88
St. Louis Roman Catholic Church 88, 89
St. Paul's Episcopal Cathedral 32, 33
St. Vincent de Paul Roman Catholic Church
   138, 139

Stanton Building 36
State University of New York at Buffalo 20, 21,
   100, 141
Statler Hotel 52
Statler Towers 52, 53
Statler, Ellsworth 52
Stone, Edward Durrell 21
Studebaker Company 18
Sullivan, Louis 13, 15, 22, 23
Surdam, Louis, House 146, 148, 149
Taylor, Hascal 24
Taylor, James Knox 32
Temple Beth Zion 20
Temple of Music 38, 145
Thaw, Evelyn 62
Thaw, Harry K. 62
The Midway 54–57
Theatre Place 45
Thomas Flyer automobile 17
Thomas, Parry, and McMullen Architects 138
Ticor Title Guarantee Company 34
Tiffany, Louis Comfort 45, 48
Tilden, Thomas 56
Toltz, Max 165
Torrey, Frank 82
Tracy, Francis W. 62
Tracy, Francis W., Monument (Forest Lawn) 82
Trinity Church (Boston) 76
Trinity Episcopal Church 48, 49
Tugwell, Rexford 48
Twentieth Century Club 58, 59
U.S. Army Signal Corps 82
Unitarian Universalist Church 110, 112, 113
University of Virginia 141
Upjohn, Richard 32
Vars Building 18
Vaux, Calvert 114
Wade, John J. 8, 19
Waite, Richard A. 34
Walden, Ebenezer 82
Walden–Myer Mausoleum 82, 83
Walter V. Davidson House 160, 161
Ward pumping station 90, 91
Warner, Andrew Jackson 29, 114
Watson, Stephen Van Rensselaer, House 48
Wendt Aircraft Company 134
Wendt, Henry W. 134
Wendt, Henry W., House 134, 135
Wendt, William 134
White, Stanford 13, 15, 21, 38, 60, 62, 64, 82,
   107, 114
Wicks, William Sydney 15, 36, 42, 84, 107, 138
Wilcox, Ansley 56
Wilcox, Ansley, House 56
William R. Heath House 154
Williams, Annie 60, 64
Williams, Charles H. 62, 64
Williams, George L. 60, 62, 64
Williams–Butler Mansion 15, 60–65
Williams–Pratt House 60, 66, 67
Woolworth and Knox five-and-ten-cent
   stores 70
Woolworth, Frank W. 70
World War I doughboy sculpture 88
Wright, Frank Lloyd 13, 15, 21, 98, 114,
   152–154, 159, 160
Wurlitzer pipe organ 45, 171
Yamasaki, Minoru 21

Bibliography

Banham, Reyner, et al, *Buffalo Architecture: A Guide* 1981

Brown, Richard C., *Buffalo, Lake City in Niagara Land* 1981

Buffalo and Erie County Historical Society, Publication Series, Vols. I through XXXIV

The Buffalo Blue Book 1901, 1903 – 1912, 1914-1923, 1926-1940

City of Buffalo, *Buffalo 125th Anniversary Souvenir Historical Book* 1957

City of Buffalo, Publications of the Buffalo Preservation Board

Conlin, John H., *Buffalo City Hall: Americanesque Masterpiece* 1993

English, Dale, *Buffalo and Niagara Falls Atlas* 1994

First Presbyterian Church, Buffalo, New York, *175th Anniversary • First Presbyterian Church
    • Buffalo, New York 1812/1987*, 1987

Floyd, Margaret Henderson, *Henry Hobson Richardson, A Genius for Architecture* 1997

Forest Lawn Cemetery, *The Gate*, Vol. 13, No. 1, 1997; Vol. 14, No. 1, 1998

Fox, Austin M., *Designated Landmarks of the Niagara Frontier* 1986

Fox, Austin M., *Erie County's Architectural Legacy* 1983

Gill, Brendan, *Many Masks, a Biography of Frank Lloyd Wright* 1987

Goldman, Mark, *City on the Lake, The Challenge of Change in Buffalo, New York* 1990

Goldman, Mark, *High Hopes, The Rise and Decline of Buffalo, New York* 1983

Goodyear, George F., *Society and Museum, A History of the Buffalo Society of Natural Sciences
    1861-1993 and the Buffalo Museum of Science 1928-1993*, 1994

Headrick, Maggie, and Celia Ehrlich, *Seeing Buffalo* 1978

History of Buffalo Harbor N.Y. 1798-1872

Hubbell, Mark H., *Buffalo, The City Beautiful* 1931

Landmark Society of the Niagara Frontier, *Downtown Buffalo's Heritage*

Larned, J. N., *A History of Buffalo* 1911

Leary, Thomas E., and Elizabeth C. Sholes, *Buffalo's Pan-American Exposition* 1998

Leary, Thomas E., and Elizabeth C. Sholes, *Buffalo's Waterfront* 1997

Lindberg, Olga, *Family Life in Early Buffalo* 1975

Lowe, David Garrard, *Stanford White's New York* 1992

McMillan, Louise, *A Field Guide to the Architecture and History of Allentown* 1987

Mead, Gerald C., Jr., *E. B. Green, Buffalo's Architect* 1997

New York Landmarks Conservancy, *Common Bond*, Vol. 12, 1996; Vol. 13, 1997; Vol. 14, 1998

Papademetriou, Peter C., *Kleinhans Music Hall, The Saarinens in Buffalo, 1940 –
    A Streamline Vision* 1990

Preservation Coalition of Erie County, *Preservation Report*, Vol. 11, 1989; Vol. 15, 1993;
    Vol. 16, 1994; Vol. 19, 1995; Vol. 21, 1997

Progress of Empire State Company, *A History of Buffalo* 1911

Reisem, Richard O., *A Field Guide to Forest Lawn Cemetery* 1998

Reisem, Richard O., *Forest Lawn Cemetery • Buffalo History Preserved* 1996

Rentz, Robert J., *A City Within a City, History of Kensington Section of the City of Buffalo* 1946

Severance, Frank, *Picture Book of Earlier Buffalo* 1912

Shaver, Peter D., *The National Register of Historic Places in New York State* 1993

Shay, Felix, *Elbert Hubbard of East Aurora* 1926

Shelton, B. K., *Buffalo in the 1890s: Reformers in Search of Yesterday* 1976

Travel Lite Associates, *Walk Buffalo* 1996

Via, Marie, and Marjorie Searl, *Head, Heart and Hand: Elbert Hubbard and the Roycrofters* 1994

Welch, Samuel M., *Recollections of Buffalo* 1891

Western New York Heritage Foundation, *Buffalo Homes* 1970

Western New York Heritage Institute, *Western New York Heritage* 1997 to 1999

Whiffen, Marcus, *American Architecture Since 1780*, 1969

White, James J., Jr., *135 Linwood* 1991

Young, Sue Miller, *A History of the Town of Amherst, New York 1818-1965*, 1965

Acknowledgments

This book was initiated through the encouragement of Albert L. Michaels, who found enthusiastic grant support from Peter and Elizabeth C. Tower. With similar lively interest, Vincent M. Cooke, S.J., and Joseph F. Bieron of Canisius College undertook administrative and marketing efforts. Andy Olenick and I are further indebted to many others who contributed selflessly. We thank, in addition to the above-mentioned persons, all of the following:

Administration: Janet Leone, Patty Shelley.

Coordination: Sherri Olenick.

Site selection: Ansie Baird, Mrs. Robert W. Colby, Judy Benjamin Goodyear, Frederic K. and Marie Houston, Mrs. Irvine Kittinger.

Research: Bette A. Rupp, Stephanie Soehnlein, Cynthia M. Van Ness.

Site information: Dean H. Jewett, Alison Fleischmann Kimberly, Daniel I. Larkin, William Menshon, Arlene Moch, George Molnar, Charles Rand Penney, Lisa A. Seivert, June F. Lippert.

Historic Visual Material: David P. Campbell.

Claude Bragdon Research: Jean France.

Text Review: John H. Conlin, Cynthia Howk, Josef Johns, Samuel W. McCune, Paul Redding, Mary Rech Rockwell, Fred R. Whaley, Jr.

Richard O. Reisem
September, 1999

Following page:
The Niagara Mohawk Building with its white-glazed terra cotta facade takes on a beautiful glow at sunset,